MEAL PREP

The No BS Meal Prep Guide to Batch Cooking and Healthy Eating for Beginners – Meal Prep, Grab and Go

Sarah Baron

D1254229

Copyright Legal Information

Table of Contents

Meal Prep Snack Recipes 113

Meal Prep Smoothie and Juice Recipes 123

Note from the Author

Meal prepping is often a tedious chore. Who wants to be cooking and prepping meals all day on a Saturday or Sunday anyways? Isn't it just easier to go out to eat during the week?

I think the reason why you got this book is because you believe in the delay of gratification. That a little bit of hard work now will lead to a less stressful week and a more beautiful you. By taking the time to create your meals for the coming work week, you can save money and eat healthier.

In my book, I have carefully selected recipes that are easy to prepare, contains simple ingredients, and provides healthy yet tasty options. Each recipe provides measurements, portion serving sizes, and the prep time so it will help you plan accordingly. I certainly hope that the recommendations and recipes in this book will help you build a healthier meal-planning habit. Meal prepping can be fun, enjoyable and hassle free! The food that is from your meal prep can also be delicious, even after being in the refrigerator or freezer.

I hope my book will bring the joy back into meal prepping. Happy cooking!

What is Meal Prep?

Meal Prep is a routine where you create a set menu for yourself, and prepare the meals ahead of time. This means scheduling and planning time to prep and cook several meals, packing them, and having them ready to grab and go. There are two different types of meal prep:

Long term meal prep: This type of meal prep means prepping your meals three+ days in advance. Most people organize an afternoon on their days off from work to purchase all the ingredients they need, prep and cook everything, and store them in glasses boxes, resealable plastic bags, or other containers. This way, they have food to take for lunch for their work or school week. This type of meal prep takes more time and more effort, but the rewards are great as you don't have to think of your cook for three to seven days.

Short term meal prep: This type of meal prep means anything less than two days. Some people organize their breakfast the day before, so when they get up they turn on the toaster or oven and their food is cooking first thing. Others marinate their meats the day or two in advance so it's ready for cooking when they need it. Doing the prep work can significantly reduce your time for cooking. These are all forms of short term meal prep.

Some people choose to prepare only certain meals, such as dinner, or even all their meals including snacks and desserts. Most of us do a mix of both long term and short term meal prep.

It might sound like a daunting task to prepare your meals, but in fact, you may already be meal prepping without knowing. You might have subconsciously chose to pick up breakfast sandwiches or muffins at the grocery store thinking that you won't have time to sit down and eat breakfast in the morning. Or you might have packed some leftover dinner for lunch the next day. These are simple forms of meal prepping.

What I will teach you is to create an effective meal plan and offer you excellent meal prep recipes. You will be given the tools in this book to own your meal plan, have all the shopping completed, and feel stress-free knowing that you have all the preps done long ahead of time!

Why Meal Prep?

Meal prepping is one of the best ways to feed yourself and your family healthy foods every day. Time is often short when you're dealing with your own schedule and your kid's schedule. Cooking is often a low priority for us.

Here are some of the benefits of meal prepping:

Save Time: Schedule conflicts and last minute items always come up in our busy lives. It's not always possible to make dinner right before dinner time. If you can prep the meals ahead of time and during time that you're free, then organizing your schedule becomes that much easier.

Save Money: If you know exactly what you're going to be making, then you can grocery shop according to your plan. Buying bulk and buying when items are on sale will help you save a fortune!

Portion Control: By measuring out all your calories and portion ahead of time and putting them in a box, you know exactly how much you will be eating. Through testing, you will know how much will fill you up and give you the nutrition that you need.

Gives you a more organized life: Some days you have a million things to do, while other days its freedom for hours and hours. If your meals are prepped during your free time, then there's no hassle for needing to make food on your busy days. This will reduce stress and give you one less thing to worry about.

Eat Healthier: Often it's because we have no other options that we stop ourselves at a fast food joint or vending machine. These high sugar and high fat meals should not belong in your system. Once you have mastered prepping your healthy snacks and meals, these unhealthy choices will no longer be needed.

Meal Prep Principles for a Healthy Lifestyle

When meal prepping, it's important to keep in mind that we are aiming for a healthy lifestyle. Having healthy, balanced meals will help you tremendously in keep high energy and spirits. We also want meal prepping to be easy, and sometimes even fun! Here are some principles that I would recommend following to keep meal prepping as simple as possible:

1. **Keep it Simple!**

Meal prepping can be difficult for those who have never done it before. It's best to select meals that are easy to make and enjoy. There's no reason to complicate a new thing. In this cookbook, you'll find that most recipes contain 6 to 9 easy to find ingredients. There are also a full chapter on smoothies that can substitute as quick meals. Start with the essentials that you are familiar to cook, such as chicken or beef. Once you master one set of ingredients, try to add 1 or 2 additional ingredients or flavoring to spice thing sup. Eventually you can morph your own recipes and add them to your weekly meal plans.

2. **Batch Cooking**

Batch cooking means cooking a large amount of the recipes in one go. It means making 10 or more portions at a time so that you can enjoy some now and freeze the rest for later in the week. Though it seems like it's a lot of work, it is actually extremely beneficial because you can get all the cooking out of the way for days, if not weeks! Sometimes when you don't time to cook, you can open your fridge or freezer, pick something that you've previously prepared, and heat it up. Recipes like our homemade granola and low fat brownies can serve as quick snacks that you can take on the go instead of store-bought items. For me, I really like batch making smoothies that can serve as my breakfast for many days.

3. **Multiple Usage of Recipes**

Many of my recipes here can be used in a variety of ways to make different meals. This will help eliminate the boredom of eating similar meals over and over again. For example, the turkey from the turkey lettuce wrap can be used to make sandwiches or can be added to soup. Similar ingredients can be used to replace each other. There are unlimited possibilities to mix and match!

4. Freshness of Ingredients

Vegetables and fruits are the hardest to keep fresh because they are easily perishable. Just because you are meal prepping doesn't mean that you'll lose all the nutrients from the lack of freshness and the deep freezes. As long as you purchase your foods fresh and then use them as soon as possible. Most of the nutrients can be kept, and this will help you with your pursue of a healthier lifestyle.

5. Get a notebook, Write it down

In my busy life, I have a hard time keeping track of everything that's going on in my mind. My best and favorite tool is a small notebook. I can easily carry it around with me, add items to it, and remind myself what tasks I have to do that day. You can also download a note app on your iphone to use. The point of having this is so you can write down all the meal preps you want to create for this week, and all the ingredients you'll need for it. You can even plan the day and time your meal prep will take place! By having this list, you'll never have to go to the supermarket twice because you forgot something. Time is of the essence!

Principles of Containers

If you don't have grab and go containers, you can't meal prep. Having the right containers will help you portion properly, as well as maintain the texture and flavor of your food. Proper containers will help reduce the air exposure of your food, thus keeping the high quality of your meals. Here's what we should look for in our grab and go containers.

- **Stackable**

Most of our kitchens have only so much space. It's important to be able to stack your containers whether they are full or empty. This will help you on space management.

- **Leakproof**

Many poorly made containers leak out of their lids, especially when they are flipped upside down or on its side. There's no worst feeling than finding out that your bag is soaked from the juices of your lunch. That will definitely kill your appetite for your meal! It is best to do your own testing by shaking the container, and flipping them on its side to check to leaks.

- **Microwave, dishwasher and freezer safe**

Your containers will go through the freeze cycle as it waits for you in the refrigerator, then it will go through a heat cycle in the microwave as you heat it up. The containers have to stand up to these changes in temperature frequently. To save time, it's good to purchase containers that are dishwasher safe too.

- **Sturdiness & Material**

Some cheaper manufacturers use cheap plastic that can easily be damaged. Often times they last maybe 3-6 months before they fall apart. Invest in high quality, glass or hard plastic containers that will last you 3-5 years. Some containers have been known to last for 10+ years if kept properly!

Avoid Freezing These Foods

Meal preps often involve freezing foods if they are to be kept for longer than 2 days in the refrigerator. Frozen foods can be kept for 2-3 weeks if necessary, thus giving you the opportunity to have meals further down the road. However, there is a short list of foods that should not be frozen. These foods usually taste different and do not keep its original texture when thawed.

- Cooked pasta
- Cooked Eggs
- Milk-based Sauces
- Cheese or crumb toppings for casseroles
- Mayonnaise
- Fried Foods
- Salad Dressing
- Raw vegetables (celery, lettuce, cabbage, etc.)

Meal Prep Day

It's time to choose a meal prep day! Most people choose Saturday or Sunday as their meal prep day because it works well with their schedules. Meal prep day doesn't have to be complicated if you have a good plan of action in place. Sometimes, if your time on your days off are limited, it's a good idea to invest in a slow cooker or Instant Pot. This is where you can throw all the ingredients in and let it cook itself! Meal Prep day usually only involves a long morning or the afternoon to complete. You can then enjoy the rest of the day doing the things you want to do.

Here is what a simple meal prep day look like. This is all dependent on what meals are being made. It will take longer for more complexed dishes. Adjust as you like.

Step 1: Meal Planning

It's time to select the meal(s) that you will prep. Figure out how many meals you need to create, and what variations of meal you are making. For example, if you plan to make Banana Pancakes for breakfast, figure out how many days you want to eat it for, what alternatives you want to make, and what ingredients you need. Make a whole shopping list a day or two before you do the actual shopping. Be sure to check your own pantry or fridge for ingredients you may already have.

Time Required: Approximately 20-30 minutes

Step 2: Purchase your Ingredients

Once you've settled on the meal prep, it's time to go shopping! Assuming that you have a full list of ingredients you need, go to your markets of choice and start picking. It might be best to pick up more of one thing for bulk buy deals (see principle #2). This way you have the ingredients already for your next meal prep. Do your best to keep with your list because it's easy to stray into the unhealthy food aisles!

Time Required: Approximately 1-2 hours

Step 3: Organize your Ingredients

After returning home with all your purchases, it's time to put them in the right places. Depending on when you are going to meal prep, you will have to make decisions on whether to store the meats in the fridge or freezer. It is best to meal prep the day of or the day after to ensure the freshness of your ingredients.

Time Required: Approximately 15 minutes

Step 4: Prepare for Cooking

It is time to cook. Firstly prepare all the ingredients and measure out all the portions. Have your kitchen equipment ready to cut, slice, measure, and stir. Marinate any meats or fish, and get the veggies washed and chopped. Cooking is easiest when all you have to do is throw everything in.

Time Required: Approximately 30-45 minutes (Dependent on Recipes)

Step 5: Cooking time

This is the easy part if you did the prep work well. If you are using a slow cooker, then throw all your ingredients in and let it work! Slow cookers can take 4-6 hours to cook a dish, so wait and enjoy. If you are doing traditional cooking, then follow the instructions and get all the dishes hot and ready for storage.

Time Required: Approximately 30-45 minutes (Dependent on Recipes)

Step 6: Prepare sauces and dressing

If you have a salad or if you are making curry chicken, then making the sauce is necessary. It's easy to follow the recipe and have these sides completed within 15-20 mins. You can also store them away first before your main courses are complete.

Time Required: Approximately 15-20 minutes (Dependent on Recipes)

Step 7: Putting it all together

Once everything is cooked, it's time to put everything together and box it all up. Divide the portions evenly for storage in the fridge or freezer. For bigger portion sizes, you may want to consider two boxes, or one large container. Considerations should also be made for wet foods and dry foods, as those should be stored separately until eating time.

Time Required: Approximately 20-30 minutes

Meal Prep Breakfast Recipes

Maple Pecan Overnight Oats

Prep Time: 10 min
Servings: 1

Ingredients:

- 1/2 cup rolled oats
- 1 tablespoon chia seeds
- 3/4 cup almond milk
- 1 tablespoon plain yogurt

- 1/2 teaspoon honey
- 1/8 teaspoon pure vanilla extract
- 2 pinches cinnamon

For the Toppings:

- 1 banana, sliced
- 1 tablespoon pecan, chopped

- 2 teaspoons maple Syrup
- 1 teaspoon ground flaxseed

Instructions:

1. In a small bowl mix together all ingredients, cover, and refrigerate for at least 5 hours or overnight.

2. The next day, or just before serving, add the toppings.

Homemade Granola

Cook Time: 1 hour 15 min
Servings: 12

Ingredients:

- 3 1/2 cups oats rolled
- 1 cup almonds raw, sliced
- 1 cup cashews or walnuts or pecans
- 1 cup unsweetened coconut flakes
- 1/2 cup sunflower seeds raw
- 1/2 cup pumpkin seeds raw
- 2 teaspoons cinnamon ground
- 1 1/2 teaspoons ginger ground
- 1/2 teaspoon nutmeg ground
- 6 tablespoons butter unsalted
- 1/2 cup honey
- 2 teaspoons pure vanilla extract
- 1/2 teaspoon salt

Instructions:

1. Preheat the oven to 250 F. Cover a rectangular baking sheet with parchment paper.
2. Mix the dry oats, almonds, cashews, coconut, seeds and spices together in a large mixing bowl.
3. Heat the butter and honey together in a small saucepan over low heat and stir in the vanilla and salt.
4. Pour the hot mixture over the dry ingredients and stir with a spatula until everything is evenly coated.
5. Spread mixture onto prepared pan in one even layer. Bake for 75 minutes.
6. Let the granola cool – it will crisp up as it cools. When it is ready, break it up into smaller pieces and store in an airtight container at room temperature for up to 2 weeks.

Blueberry Breakfast Bars

Cook Time: 1 hour 15 min
Servings: 16

Ingredients:

- 1 1/2 cups rolled oats
- 1/2 cup dried blueberries
- 1/2 cup pistachios, shelled
- 1/3 ground flaxseed
- 1/3 cup walnuts
- 1/3 cup pumpkin seeds
- 1/4 cup sunflower seeds
- 1/3 cup honey
- 1/4 cup unsweetened apple sauce
- 1 cup almond butter (or any other nut butter)

Instructions:

1. Line a medium sized baking pan with parchment paper. Make sure the paper extends out over the edges for easy removal later.
2. Combine the first 8 ingredients into a large bowl.
3. Stir in almond butter, or any other nut butter, until well combined.
4. Tip the mixture into the pan and press it flat, distributing the mixture as evenly as possible.
5. Freeze for about an hour. When ready, lift the mixture out of the pan by gripping the edges of the parchment paper. Gently peel paper off and slice the slab into bars.
6. Store in an airtight container in the freezer.

Brownie Granola Bars

Cook Time: 45 min
Servings: 12

Ingredients:

- 1.5 cups rolled oats (GF for gluten free eaters)
- 1 cup raw nuts, roughly chopped (I used 1/2 cup almonds, 1/2 cup pecans)
- 1 cup raw walnuts
- 2 cups pitted dates, soaked for 10 minutes in warm water, then drained
- 3/4 cup cocoa or cacao powder
- 1/4 cup natural salted almond butter (or peanut butter)
- 1/4 cup agave nectar, maple syrup, or honey if not vegan

Instructions:

1. Process walnuts in a food processor until it is crumbly. Set aside.
2. Add dates and process until it forms a dough-like consistency. Add walnut meal and cocoa or cacao powder and process to combine. Transfer mixture to a large mixing bowl and add the oats and nuts. Stir to combine.
3. Warm honey and almond butter in a small skillet over medium heat until pourable. Pour over brownie mixture and then stir through with a spoon.
4. Transfer to square pan lined with plastic wrap.
5. Cover mixture with parchment paper and press down firmly to even out the top. Use a spatula to smooth out the surface. Freeze for 15-20 minutes to harden.
6. Lift bars from pan and cut into 12 even bars Store in an airtight container in the freezer or fridge.

Maple Walnut Breakfast Cookies

Cook Time: 20 min
Servings: 20

Ingredients:

- 1 cup whole-wheat flour
- ¾ cup oats rolled
- ½ teaspoon baking soda
- ¼ teaspoon salt
- ¼ cup applesauce
- 3 tablespoons pure maple syrup
- 2 tablespoons butter softened but not melted
- 1 egg
- 1/2 teaspoon pure vanilla extract
- 1/2 cup walnut chopped

Instructions:

1. Preheat oven to 375 F and grease a baking sheet.
2. Whisk together the flour, oats, baking soda, and salt.
3. In a separate bowl, using an electric mixer beat the applesauce, maple syrup, butter, egg, and vanilla.
4. While beating the mixture on a low speed add the dry ingredients until well blended.
5. Fold in the nuts with a spatula.
6. Drop onto prepared cookie sheet with a spoon. Bake for 8 - 9 minutes or until they start to brown.

Banana Pancakes

Cook Time: 20 min
Servings: 4

Ingredients:

- 2 cups whole-wheat flour
- 2 teaspoons baking powder
- 1 ½ teaspoons baking soda
- ½ teaspoon salt
- 1 tablespoon honey
- 2 eggs lightly beaten
- 1 ¾ cups milk
- 2 tablespoons butter unsalted, melted, + butter for frying
- 2 bananas mashed
- pure maple syrup for serving

Instructions:

1. In a large bowl, whisk together the flour, baking powder, baking soda, and salt.
2. Make a well (hole) in the center of the flour mixture and pour in the honey, eggs, milk, and 2 tablespoons of melted butter. Whisk together thoroughly, but do not overmix.
3. Gently fold the mashed bananas into the batter with a spatula.
4. Heat a griddle or sauté pan over medium-high heat. Swirl enough butter around the pan until it is well coated. Add pancake batter using a soup ladle.
5. When the pancakes have begun to turn brown on the bottom, flip them over to cook the other side.
6. Serve with warm maple syrup and a side of fruit or freeze to have the rest of the week

Whole-Wheat Crepes

Cook Time: 25 min
Servings: 4

Ingredients:

- 3 eggs
- 1 cup whole-wheat flour
- 1 cup milk
- 3/4 cup water
- 1 tablespoon honey
- 1 teaspoon vanilla
- 1/4 teaspoon salt
- 1 tablespoon butter melted, + extra for cooking

Instructions:

1. Put all ingredients in blender and mix well. Let the batter rest for about 15 minutes.
2. Melt and spread some butter in a frying pan over medium heat.
3. Pour enough batter onto one side of the pan and swirl it to thinly and evenly cover the pan.
4. With a cooking spatula, push down the edges of the crepe.
5. When the crepe is golden brown on the bottom, carefully flip it over.
6. Fry for 1 more minute on the other side and then plate the crepe.
7. Serve with fruit and maple syrup.

Apple Sauce Waffles

Cook Time: 30 min
Servings: 2

Ingredients:

- 1 3/4 cup whole-wheat flour
- 2 teaspoons baking powder
- 1 teaspoon cinnamon
- 1/2 teaspoon salt
- 1 1/2 cups milk
- 4 tablespoons butter melted
- 1/2 cup applesauce
- 3 eggs separated

Instructions:

1. Preheat the waffle iron. In a medium mixing bowl, whisk the flour, baking powder, cinnamon and salt.
2. Make a well in the center of the dry ingredients and pour in the milk, melted butter, applesauce, and egg yolks. Mix until well combined and set aside.
3. Use an electric mixer to beat the egg whites until stiff peaks form. Carefully fold the egg whites into the batter 1/3 at a time until there are no more white streaks.
4. Follow manufacturer's instructions with your waffle iron to make the batter into waffles.

Assorted Muffins

Cook Time: 25 min
Servings: 12

Ingredients:

- 1 1/2 cups whole-wheat flour
- 1/2 teaspoon salt
- 2 teaspoons baking powder
- 1/2 teaspoon cinnamon
- 1/8 teaspoon nutmeg

- 2 eggs
- 2 tablespoons honey
- 1 teaspoon pure vanilla extract
- 1/4 cup coconut oil or other oil of your choice
- 3/4 cup apple juice or orange juice

Fillings:

- Blueberries
- Diced strawberries
- Peeled and diced pears
- Applesauce
- Either diced or mashed up bananas and chopped walnuts

- Raisins and chopped pecans (I add an extra pinch of cinnamon to the muffins with this filling)
- Grated carrot and chopped walnuts
- Orange or lemon zest (only add 1/4 to 1/2 teaspoon of zest per individual muffin)
- A mix of dried fruit bits
- Jelly

Instructions:

1. Heat oven to 400 F.
2. In a large bowl whisk the flour, salt, baking powder, cinnamon and nutmeg.
3. Make a well in the center of the flour mixture and pour in the eggs, honey, vanilla, oil and orange juice. Mix the dry and wet ingredients together – do not overmix.
4. Line a muffin pan with liners and fill 2/3 to 3/4 of the way full with batter. In each muffin cup, add different fillings to the batter.
5. Sprinkle 1 – 2 teaspoons of whatever you would like onto the top of each and then gently stir with a fork.
6. Bake for 10 – 15 minutes or until a toothpick comes out clean. Serve warm or at room temperature or freeze some to eat later.

Whole-Wheat Popovers

Cook Time: 20 min
Servings: 6

Ingredients:

- 2 eggs at room temperature
- 2/3 cup milk at room temperature (I used 2%)
- 2 tablespoons butter melted
- 2/3 cup whole-wheat flour
- 1/8 teaspoon salt

Instructions:

1. Preheat the oven to 425 F and grease a non-stick muffin pan.
2. Whisk together the eggs, milk, and butter. Add the flour and salt into the egg mixture and continue to whisk until everything is well combined.
3. Pour the batter into the prepared muffin cups until they are at least three-quarters full.
4. Bake for 14 – 16 minutes or until the popovers are puff up and golden brown. Do not open the oven and let the heat out while baking.
5. Once they are done pierce the popovers with a skewer or toothpick to let the steam out. Trapped steam could cause the inside to become soggy.
6. Store in an airtight container and leave them at room temperature.

Banana Bread

Cook Time: 1 hour
Servings: 6

Ingredients:

- 2 ¼ cup whole-wheat flour
- ¾ teaspoon baking soda
- ¼ teaspoon salt
- 3 bananas ripe, mashed
- ¼ cup plain yogurt
- ¼ cup honey
- 2 eggs
- 1/3 cup coconut oil (or another mild oil of your choice)
- 1 teaspoon pure vanilla extract

Instructions:

1. Preheat oven to 350 F and grease a pan.
2. Whisk together the flour, baking soda, and salt.
3. In a separate bowl mix mashed bananas with yogurt, honey, eggs, oil, and vanilla.
4. Fold the banana mixture into the flour mixture until blended. Do not overmix.
5. Pour batter into prepared pan.
6. Bake large loaf for 40 – 50 minutes or until it comes clean with a toothpick.

Cinnamon Raisin Bread

Cook Time: 4 hour 15 min
Servings: 1 loaf

Ingredients:

- 3 cups whole-wheat flour
  2 teaspoons cinnamon
  ½ teaspoon salt
  1 cup water warmed

½ cup coconut oil
4 tablespoons honey
2 teaspoons active dry yeast
1 cup raisins

Instructions:

1. Follow your bread machine's directions for making a whole-wheat raisin loaf.

2. Take out the bread 10 minutes before the standard end time for a lighter crust.

Whole-Wheat Cinnamon Rolls

Cook Time: 1 hour 45 min
Servings: 6

For the Dough:

- 8 tablespoons butter
- 2/3 cup milk
- 2 tablespoons pure maple syrup
- 2 1/4 teaspoons active dry yeast
- 3 cups whole-wheat flour + 2 tablespoons for rolling out the dough
- 1/2 teaspoon salt
- 2 eggs

For the Filling:

- 4 tablespoons butter
- 2/3 cup pecans crushed
- 1/4 cup pure maple syrup
- 3 tablespoons cinnamon

Instructions:

1. In a small sauce pan melt the butter for the dough. Remove from heat and stir in the milk, syrup and yeast. Set aside.
2. In a large stand mixer fitted with a dough hook, mix together the flour and salt. Drop in the eggs and the butter/milk mixture and mix to combine. If very sticky to the touch add more flour (a tablespoon at a time) until it forms one ball that can easily be handled. Transfer the dough ball to a bowl that's been greased with butter, cover with a clean dish towel and let rise on the counter for at least 30 minutes.
3. Meanwhile, melt the butter for the filling then stir in the pecans, maple syrup, and cinnamon.
4. When ready, roll out the dough onto a floured surface to a rectangle about 14X9" in size. Cut and pinch together pieces if needed to make an even rectangle.
5. Evenly brush the filling mixture over top then, starting on the long side, and roll over the dough until the seam side is facing down. Carefully cut pieces between 3/4" and 1" thick and place cut side up in greased baking dish. Reshape as needed. Let rise for another 30 minutes. (At this point you could cover with plastic wrap and store in fridge overnight.)
6. Preheat the oven to 375 degrees F. Bake until golden brown, about 25 minutes.

Stuffed Peppers

Cook Time: 35 min
Servings: 8

Ingredients:

- 4 large bell peppers, whatever color you like
- 9 large eggs
- 1/2 cup fully cooked breakfast potatoes*
- 1/2 cup cooked quinoa
- 1/2 cup black beans
- 1/2 cup chopped spinach leaves
- 1/3 cup shredded cheese, plus more for topping if desired
- 1 teaspoon salt
- 1/4 teaspoon black pepper

Instructions:

1. Pre-heat the oven to 400 degrees Fahrenheit. Cut the peppers in half and remove the seeds. You can either cut them in half width-wise or length-wise but they will probably stand up better if you cut them width-wise. Place the peppers on a baking sheet and bake for 5 minutes.
2. Crack the eggs into a large mixing bowl and beat with a fork. Add the remaining ingredients and mix until combined.
3. Remove the peppers from the oven and spoon the egg mixture into each pepper, amount will depend on how big your peppers are. Sprinkle the top of each pepper with cheese and place back in the oven and bake peppers until eggs are set, about 20 minutes. Serve eggs immediately and top with chopped herbs if desired.

Sweet Potato Hash

Cook Time: 30 min
Servings: 4

Ingredients:

- 2 tablespoons olive oil
- 1 tablespoon minced garlic
- 1 large sweet potato, peeled
- 1 red pepper, finely diced
- ½ yellow onion, finely diced
- 4 chicken sausages, precooked
- 4 cups kale, deboned
- salt and pepper, to taste
- 2 tablespoons balsamic vinegar

Instructions:

1. Place 1 tablespoon of olive oil in a nonstick skillet and turn to medium/high heat.
2. Add in sweet potato, onion, red pepper, and sliced chicken sausages. Sauté for about 5-7 minutes or until onions become fragrant and translucent.
3. Add in kale and a tablespoon more olive oil. Sauté until kale has wilted. Season with salt, pepper, and 2 tablespoons of balsamic vinegar.

Meal Prep Soup & Salad Recipes

Rainbow Soba Noodle Salad

Cook Time: 30 min
Servings: 4

For the salad:
- 6 ounces soba noodles
- 2 cups julienned carrots
- 1 1/2 cups shredded red cabbage
- 1 cup cooked edamame
- 1/2 cup thinly sliced green onion
- optional: sesame seeds for garnish

For the dressing:
- 3 tablespoons tamari or soy sauce
- 3 tablespoons fresh lime juice
- 2 1/2 tablespoons toasted sesame oil
- 1-2 tablespoons honey, agave or brown rice syrup
- 1-2 garlic cloves, pressed
- 1-2 teaspoons tahini
- 1/2 teaspoon ginger paste
- 1/2 teaspoon sriracha

Instructions:
1. In a small mixing bowl, whisk dressing ingredients together and set aside.
2. In a large mixing bowl, add in all the salad ingredients except the soba noodles. Toss gently to mix. Set aside.
3. Cook soba noodles according to package directions. Drain and rinse noodles under cold water until noodles are cold to the touch. Add noodles to the salad, and gently toss. Season with salt and pepper to taste.
4. Portion out salad and pour dressing over when ready to eat.

Mediterranean Quinoa Salad

Cook Time: 50 min
Servings: 8

Ingredients:

- 2 cups 25%-less-sodium chicken broth
- 1 cup quinoa, uncooked
- 1 cup cherry tomatoes, halved
- 1 small English cucumber, chopped
- 1 small red onion, cut crosswise in half, thinly sliced
- 10 cups torn romaine lettuce

For the Dressing:

- 1/2 cup sundried tomatoes, roughly chopped
- 1/2 cup extra virgin olive oil
- 1 tablespoon lemon juice
- 1 teaspoon dry oregano
- 1/2 cup feta cheese, crumbled
- Salt and Pepper to taste

Instructions:

1. Bring broth and quinoa to boil in saucepan on high heat; simmer on medium-low heat 15 min. or until liquid is absorbed. Set aside to cool.
2. In a medium bowl, combine all the dressing ingredients and whisk well to combine.
3. Combine tomatoes, cucumbers and onions in medium bowl. Add 1/4 cup dressing and toss to coat.
4. To serve, layer a serving bowl with lettuce and top with quinoa, and vegetable mixture. Drizzle remaining dressing.

Protein Packed Salad

Prep Time: 30 min
Servings: 2

Ingredients:

- 2 cups kale, stems removed and chopped
- 2 cups broccoli, chopped
- 2 cups snap peas
- 2 cups tofu, sliced and pan fried
- 1 cup almonds, roasted
- 1 cup dried apricots, sliced
- 1/2 cup ginger sesame dressing (or your favorite dressing)

Instructions:

1. Divide your dressing into two mason jars.
2. In each jar, layer the ingredients, starting with items that are lease likely to wilt:
   o Snap peas
   o Broccoli
   o Kale
   o Almonds
   o Apricots
   o Tofu
3. Seal jar and store in fridge. To serve, shake the jar to distribute the dressing.

Chickpea and Pasta Soup

Cook Time: 45 min
Servings: 4

Ingredients:

- 2 tablespoons olive oil
- 1/2 sweet onion, diced
- 2 garlic cloves, minced
- 1/4 teaspoon salt
- 1/4 teaspoon pepper
- 2 tablespoon tomato paste
- 2 tablespoons brown sugar
- 2 teaspoons dried oregano
- 1/8 teaspoon crushed red pepper flakes
- 1 (28-ounce) can whole peeled tomatoes
- 1 cup tomato puree
- 2 cups low-sodium chicken or vegetable stock
- 1 (15-ounce) can chickpeas, drained and rinsed
- 1 cup whole wheat pasta, cooked
- 1 cup freshly grated parmesan cheese, plus more for topping
- chopped fresh parsley + basil topping

Instructions:

2. Heat a large pot over medium-low heat and add the olive oil. Stir in the onion, garlic, salt, pepper, and cook, stirring occasionally, until the onion turns translucent.
   Stir in the tomato paste, sugar, oregano and red pepper flakes, cooking for another 1 to 2 minutes. Make sure to stir occasionally.
3. Add in the whole peeled tomatoes and cook until softens. Break apart the tomatoes with a wooden spoon, then add the puree and stock.
4. Cover soup and cook on medium heat for 10 to 15 minutes.
5. Add the chickpeas and cook for 10 minutes.
6. Stir in the parmesan cheese until melted and season additionally with salt and pepper if needed.
7. To serve, ladle soup over cooked pasta and top with cheese and chopped fresh herbs.

Healthy Lasagna Soup

Cook Time: 25 min
Servings: 1

Instructions:

- 1 yellow onion, chopped
- kosher salt
- 1 lb. lean ground turkey sausage
- 4 cloves garlic, minced
- 28 oz. can crushed tomatoes or 28 oz. jar of marinara sauce
- 1 tbsp. dried oregano

- 5 c. low-sodium chicken broth
- 8 oz. lasagna noodles, broke into 2" pieces
- 2 c. low fat shredded mozzarella
- Toppings (optional):
- Grated Parmesan, for garnish
- Torn fresh basil, for garnish

Ingredients:

1. In a large skillet over medium heat, heat some oil. Sauté onions and season with salt. Cook onions until translucent, then add sausage and cook well done. Drain the excess fat and add to a soup pot.
2. In the pot, add garlic and stir until fragrant. Tip in a can of crushed tomatoes and the dried oregano.

3. Pour in chicken broth and bring to a simmer.
4. Add lasagna noodles and cook, stirring occasionally, until pasta is al dente.
5. Sprinkle in mozzarella and stir, letting the cheese melt into soup.
6. To serve, garnish with Parm and basil.

Butternut Squash and Turkey Chili

Cook Time: 40 min
Servings: 6

Ingredients:

- 1/2 tablespoon olive oil
- 1 medium onion, diced
- 4 large garlic cloves, minced
- 2 teaspoons ground turmeric
- 1 teaspoon ground cumin
- 1 teaspoon chili powder
- 1/4 teaspoon cayenne pepper
- 1/4 teaspoon cinnamon
- 1 teaspoon sea salt
- 1/2 teaspoon ground black pepper, to taste
- 1 pound ground turkey
- 1 medium butternut squash, peeled, seeded and chopped (about 5 cups)
- 4 cups low-sodium vegetable broth
- 1 can diced tomatoes
- 1 can light coconut milk
- 1/2 cup dried red lentils, rinsed
- 3 tablespoons tomato paste
- 2-3 teaspoons apple cider vinegar
- 1-2 cups chopped kale or spinach
- Chopped cilantro and sliced green onions, for garnish
- Cooked brown rice or quinoa (optional)

Instructions:

1. Add oil to a large pot over medium heat. Add onion and garlic and sauté for 3-5 minutes.
2. Add ground turkey and cook until brown, about 5-7 minutes. Break up the meat while cooking.
3. Add spices (turmeric, cumin, chili powder, cayenne pepper, cinnamon, sea salt and pepper) and cook for an additional minute.
4. Add butternut squash chunks, veggie broth, tomatoes, coconut milk, red lentils, and tomato paste and apple cider vinegar to the pot. Stir to combine.
5. Bring mixture to a boil. Once bubbling, reduce heat to medium and simmer, stirring occasionally. Once the butternut squash is tender and the lentils are cooked, reduce heat to low.
6. Add in kale or spinach, stir to combine. Simmer until the greens have wilted.
7. To serve, divide the chili into bowls and top each bowl with fresh cilantro and green onions.

Meal Prep Bowl Recipes

Chicken Fajita Bowls

Cook Time: 30 min
Servings: 4

Ingredients:

- 2 chicken breasts
- 1 tablespoon olive oil
- Salt & pepper
- 3/4 cup basmati rice (uncooked)

- 2 bell peppers, sliced into strips
- 2 tablespoons red onion, diced
- 1 cup corn kernels

For the Vinaigrette

- 1 teaspoon chili powder
- 1/2 teaspoon paprika
- 1/2 teaspoon ground cumin
- 1 tablespoon sugar

- 1 tablespoon lime juice
- 1/4 teaspoon salt
- 3 tablespoons olive oil
- 3 tablespoons white wine vinegar

Instructions:

1. Pre-heat oven to 425 F.
2. Place the chicken breasts in a small baking dish. Sprinkle with salt and pepper, and drizzle olive oil over the chicken. Repeat on the other side.
3. Bake chicken for 20 minutes, making sure to flip the chicken half way until meat has cooked through.
4. Allow to rest for 10 more minutes before slicing.
5. Cook the rice according to package directions. Allow to cool.
6. Meanwhile, whisk together the vinaigrette ingredients.
7. To assemble, spoon the rice into a large bowl. Top with bell peppers, red onion and corn. Toss to coat everything completely.
8. Portion the rice and vegetables, and top with a portion of chicken.
9. Refrigerate until you are ready to serve.

Chicken and Veggie Bowls

Cook Time: 40 min
Servings: 4

Ingredients:

- 1 1/2 cup cooked quinoa
- 1 1/2 cup cooked brown rice
- 1/4 cup olive oil
- 2 cups asparagus, chopped

- 2 cups broccoli florets
- 2 cups cauliflower florets
- 4 chicken breasts
- Salt and Pepper to Taste

For the Marinade

- 1 teaspoon ground cumin
- 1 teaspoon kosher salt
- 1/2 teaspoon freshly ground black pepper
- 1/2 teaspoon smoked paprika (regular paprika works too)

- 1/2 teaspoon garlic salt
- 3-4 medium to large boneless skinless chicken breasts
- 2 limes, split

Instructions:

1. In a large sandwich bag, combine the marinade ingredients. Drop chicken breasts into the marinade and marinate for minimum 20 minutes, but best overnight.
2. Preheat the oven to 400 F and lightly grease a baking sheet.
3. In a large mixing bowl, toss the vegetables with olive oil and season to taste. Arrange vegetables in a single, even, layer on the prepared baking sheet and bake for 10-15 minutes or until vegetables are lightly browned on the edges.
4. In a large skillet, heat a tablespoon of olive oil. Pan Fry the chicken breast until fully cooked. Set aside to cool slightly before dicing the chicken into bite-sized pieces.
5. To serve, divide quinoa, brown rice, chicken, and vegetables into individual containers.

Pork Burrito Bowls

Cook Time: 2 hours 15 min
Servings: 4

Ingredients:

- 2 cups brown rice, cooked
- 1/4 cup cilantro, finely chopped
- 1 can yellow sweet corn
- 1 can black beans, rinsed and drained
- 4 cups of romaine, chopped

- 1/3 cup red onion, finely chopped
- 1/3 cup cojita cheese
- 1/2 teaspoon paprika
- 2 limes
- Salt and pepper to taste

For the Carnitas:

- 1 pound pork loin (option to use chicken breast instead)
- 1 tablespoon minced garlic
- 1 tablespoons orange juice
- 1/3 cup lime juice

- 3 teaspoon cumin
- 2 teaspoons smoked paprika
- salt and pepper, to taste
- 1/4 cup green chilies

Instructions:

1. Place pork loin and minced garlic into a crock-pot cook on high for 2-4 hours. Remove pork loin and shred with 2 forks. Place shredded pork into a large bowl and add in the rest of the carnitas ingredients. Mix well to combine.
2. In a medium sized bowl, mix the corn, red onion, cojita cheese, the juice of half a lime, and paprika.
3. In another medium bowl, toss the rice with the juice of half a lime and the chopped cilantro.
4. To assemble, line the bottom of a bowl with romaine lettuce. Top with a layer of the cilantro lime rice, carnitas, corn, and black beans. Serve with a lime wedge.

Lemongrass Meatball Bowls

Cook Time: 1 hour and 10 min
Servings: 4

Ingredients:

- 2 cups brown rice
- 2 tablespoons cilantro, finely chopped
- 2 tablespoons basil, finely chopped
- 2 tablespoons mint, finely chopped

- 2 tablespoons green onions, diced
- 1/4 cup crushed peanuts or sesame seeds
- Sriracha to taste

For the Pickled Carrots

- 1/3 cup rice vinegar
- ¼ cup coconut palm sugar
- 1 tablespoon sesame oil

- 1 teaspoon salt
- 6 carrots, cut into thin ribbons

For the Meatballs

- 1 pound ground pork
- 2 tablespoons lemongrass paste
- 4 cloves garlic, minced
- 1 tablespoon chili paste

- 1 tablespoon fish sauce
- 1 tablespoon coconut palm sugar
- 2 teaspoons cornstarch
- 1 teaspoon salt

Instructions:

1. To prepare the pickled carrots, whisk the rice vinegar, palm sugar, sesame oil, and salt together. Soak the carrots in the mixture for at least one hour.
2. While carrots are pickling, prepare the meatballs. Mix all meatball ingredients. Roll into small balls with your hands.
3. Heat a little bit of olive oil in a medium skillet over medium high heat. Add the meatballs and fry until golden brown on the outside and fully cooked on the inside.
4. To assemble the bowls, layer the carrots and meatballs over the brown rice. Top with the chopped herbs and a sprinkle of crushed peanuts. Drizzle Sriracha on top to taste.

Thai Inspired Coconut Quinoa Bowls

Cook Time: 45 min
Servings: 4

Ingredients:

- 2 cup quinoa
- 1 can coconut milk
- 1/2 cup water
- 1 large sweet potato, diced
- 2 cups carrots, diced
- 1 tablespoon minced garlic

- 2 tablespoons olive oil
- Salt and pepper, to taste
- 1/4 cup peanut butter
- 2 tablespoons crushed peanuts
- 2 tablespoons cilantro, finely chopped

For the Cabbage Slaw

- 1 cup purple cabbage, finely chopped
- 1 cup edamame
- 1 small red pepper, diced
- 1 tablespoon low-sodium tamari (or soy sauce)
- 2 tablespoons extra virgin olive oil

- 1 lime, juiced
- 1 tablespoon maple syrup
- 1/4 teaspoon garlic powder
- 1/4 teaspoon ginger powder
- 1/4 teaspoon dried orange peel

Instructions:

1. In a medium sized point, bring the water, coconut milk, and quinoa to a boil. Reduce to low and cover, cook for about 10 minutes or until all the liquid has been absorbed. Season with salt and pepper and fluff with a fork.
2. Placed diced vegetables in a large baking sheet and drizzle with olive oil. Mix in minced garlic and season with salt and pepper. Toss to coat.
3. Roast vegetables at 400 F for 25-30 minutes or until the vegetables are tender.
4. In a large bowl, add the cabbage, edamame, and red pepper. Mix the remaining cabbage slaw ingredients together. Toss gently to coat.
5. To assemble, add the coconut quinoa to the bottom of a bowl and top with roasted veggies and cabbage slaw. Finish with a sprinkle of crushed peanuts and cilantro. Drizzle over some peanut butter thinned out with olive oil.

Hawaiian Chicken Noodle Bowls

Cook Time: 2 hours
Servings: 4

Ingredients:

- 4 cups rice noodles, cooked
- 1 cup fresh pineapple, cubed
- 4 small boneless, skinless chicken breasts
- 1/2 cup pineapple juice*
- 2 tablespoons ketchup
- 1/2 teaspoon fresh ginger, grated
- 1 teaspoon garlic, minced
- 2 tablespoons low sodium tamari
- 1 tablespoon honey
- Pinch of salt
- Coconut chips
- Green onion, diced

For the Pineapple Stir Fry

- 1 tablespoon coconut oil
- 1 cup purple onion, diced (~1/2 medium onion)
- 2 large sweet peppers, diced
- 2 cups chopped kale, packed
- 1 tablespoon pineapple juice
- 1 tablespoon low sodium tamari
- 1 tablespoon chili sauce
- ½ tablespoon honey
- 1 tablespoon minced garlic

Instructions:

1. In a small bowl, whisk together the pineapple juice, ketchup, ginger, garlic, tamari, honey and salt. Place chicken breasts into a crock pot and pour sauce over. Cook chicken on high for 1.5-2 hours and shred with two forks when chicken is done.
2. Heat 1 tablespoon of coconut oil in a medium skillet. Sauté the onions and peppers until onions are almost translucent. Ad in the kale and sauté for a few more minutes.
3. In a small bowl, mix the rest of the ingredients and pour over the stir-fry. Cook for a few more minutes until sauce reduces slightly.
4. To assemble, add rice noodles to the bottom of a bowl and top with fresh pineapples and the shredded chicken. Spoon over some pineapple stir fry, making sure to get enough sauce to coat the noodles. Sprinkle over the coconut chips and green onions.

Buddha Bowls

Cook Time: 30 min
Servings: 4

Ingredients:

- 2 cups Quinoa, cooked
- 2 tablespoons sesame oil
- 2 cloves garlic, minced
- 1/4 cup green onion, minced
- 1 15 oz. can chickpeas
- 4 cups broccolini
- 1 heaping cup matchstick carrots
- 2 tablespoons tamari (soy sauce or coconut aminos)
- 1 tablespoon sriracha
- 1 tablespoon chili paste
- 1 tablespoon honey
- Crushed peanuts

For the Dressing:

- 1 cup basil, chopped (not packed)
- 1 cup flat leaf parsley, chopped (not packed)
- 1/4 cup green onion
- 1 clove garlic, minced
- 1 teaspoon apple cider vinegar
- 2 tablespoons freshly squeezed lemon juice
- 1/4 cup olive oil
- 1 cup plain non-fat Greek yogurt
- Salt and pepper, to taste
- Cayenne pepper, to taste

Instructions:

1. Place sesame oil in a large pan and heat on medium/high heat. Add in the vegetables and sauté for 3-5 minutes. When the vegetables soften slightly, add in the sauce ingredients and continue to sauté for a few minutes.
2. Add all dressing ingredients into a food processor and blend until smooth.
3. In a small bowl, whisk together the sriracha, chili paste, and honey.
4. To assemble the bowls, divide the quinoa into 4 portions. Top with the vegetable stir-fry and a dollop of the dressing. Drizzle with chili sauce and sprinkle chopped peanuts on top.

Mediterranean Chicken and Farro Bowls

Cook Time: 55 min
Servings: 4

Ingredients:

- 2 cups farro, cooked
- 2 chicken breasts
- 1 tablespoon olive oil
- 1 tablespoon balsamic vinegar
- ½ eggplant, cubed
- 1 medium zucchini, cubed

- 1 fennel bulb, cubed
- 1 tablespoon olive oil
- 1 tablespoon balsamic vinegar
- salt and pepper
- 1/4 cup feta cheese, crumbled

For the Vinaigrette

- 2 tablespoons olive oil
- 2 tablespoons balsamic vinaigrette

- ½ tablespoon maple syrup
- ¼ teaspoon Dijon mustard

Instructions:

1. Preheat the oven to 400 F. In a small baking dish, combine the oil and balsamic vinegar. Add the chicken and turn to coat. Season with salt and pepper.
2. Bake chicken for 25 minutes, making sure to flip half way. When fully cooked, set aside to cool. When chicken has cooled, cut into bite sized pieces.
3. Toss the eggplant, zucchini and fennel in the olive oil and balsamic vinegar, and then spread them out on a large parchment-lined baking sheet. Sprinkle with salt and pepper.
4. Bake vegetables for 15 minutes or until fennel is tender, make sure to stir the vegetables half way.
5. Whisk together the ingredients for the vinaigrette.
6. To assemble, divide the farro into 4 portions. Add the cooked vegetables and chicken on top of each portion. Sprinkle with feta and a drizzle of vinaigrette.

Turkey Sausage and Sweet Potato Bowls

Cook Time: 40 min
Servings: 4

Ingredients:

- 4-5 cups sweet potato cubes
- 1 tablespoon olive oil
- 1 pound Italian turkey sausage
- Mixed Vegetables

- 4-5 cups bell peppers, red onion and zucchini slices
- 1 tablespoon olive oil
- Salt and pepper

For the Sauce:

- 2 tablespoons tahini
- 1.5 tablespoons water (or more to thin out)
- 1.5 teaspoons maple syrup

- 1.5 teaspoons lemon juice
- ⅛ teaspoon salt

Instructions

1. Toss the sweet potatoes with olive oil, salt and pepper. Pre-heat oven to 425 F. Line a baking sheet with parchment. Arrange sweet potato cubes on the baking sheet, and bake for 15 minutes.
2. Give them a stir and return to the oven for another 10 or so minutes, until they are tender and can be pierced through easily.
3. Pierce sausage casing with a knife to help the steam escape. Fry on skillet over medium high heat, until cooked through. When done, slice sausage into bite sized chunks.
4. Toss veggies with olive oil and salt and pepper. Arrange in a single layer on a baking sheet and bake for 10-15 minutes, stirring the vegetables half way.
5. For the sauce, whisk together all the ingredients. Add more water to help thin out the sauce to a preferred consistency.
6. In a large bowl, toss together the sweet potatoes and vegetables. Divide into equal portions. Portion out the turkey sausage and then spoon the sauce on top.

Jerk Chicken Pasta Bowl

Cook Time: 45 min
Servings: 4

Ingredients:

- 2 cups rotini pasta, cooked
- 2 large chicken breasts
- 2 bell peppers, cut into large chunks
- 1 large zucchini, cut into large chunks
- 2 tablespoon olive oil
- 1 lime, juiced
- 1/4 cup cilantro, finely chopped
- 1 small jalapeno, seeds removed and finely chopped
- 1 clove garlic, minced
- 2 mangoes, cubed

For the Rub

- 1/2 tablespoon dried thyme leaves
- 1/2 tablespoon ground allspice
- 1 tablespoon brown sugar
- 1/2 teaspoon salt
- 1/2 teaspoon pepper
- 1/2 tablespoon garlic powder
- 1/2 teaspoon cinnamon
- Cayenne powder, to taste

Ingredients:

1. Pre-heat oven to 425 F.
2. Stir together the rub ingredients and set aside.
3. In a medium bowl, toss the chicken with half a tablespoon of olive oil and half of the lime juice. Sprinkle with half the rub and toss to coat evenly. Arrange on a baking sheet and bake for 25 minutes or until fully cooked.
4. To prepare the vegetables, toss the vegetables with half a tablespoon of olive oil, lime juice and rub. Arrange on a second baking sheet in an even layer and bake for 15 minutes or until vegetables are tender.
5. Meanwhile, toss the cooked pasta with 1 tablespoon of olive oil, cilantro, salt and pepper, and the remaining lime juice. When the chicken and vegetables are done, take them out and let them cool; slice chicken into bite-sized pieces.
6. Divide the pasta and veggies and top with the sliced chicken breast. Finish off with some fresh mango cubes.

Meal Prep Main Course Recipes

Turkey Lettuce Wraps

Cook Time: 20 min
Servings: 2

Ingredients:

- 1 1/4 pound. fat-free lean ground turkey
- 1 tablespoon olive oil
- 1 clove garlic, minced
- 1/8 teaspoon ground ginger
- 4 green onions, thinly sliced
- 1 can sliced water chestnuts, drained and coarsely chopped

- 3 tablespoon hoisin sauce
- 2 tablespoon tamari
- 1 tablespoon rice vinegar
- 2 teaspoon roasted red chili paste
- Salt and pepper to taste
- 12 Boston lettuce leaves

Instructions:

1. Heat 1 tablespoon of oil in a large nonstick skillet over medium-high heat. Add turkey, garlic and ginger to the pan and cook for about 6 minutes or until turkey is browned. Stir to crumble.
2. Combine turkey mixture, onions and chopped water chestnuts in a large bowl, stirring well, and set aside.
3. Meanwhile in a small bowl, whisk together hoisin, soy sauce, rice vinegar and roasted red chili paste and drizzle over the turkey mixture. Toss to coat completely.
4. Add about 1/4 cup turkey mixture to each lettuce leaf, serve and enjoy!

Cauliflower Fried Rice

Cook Time: 20 min
Servings: 4

Ingredients:

- 1 head cauliflower, chopped into florets
- 1 small yellow onion, finely chopped
- 1/2 cup frozen peas
- 1/2 cup carrots, cubed
- 2 eggs, beaten
- 1 tablespoon sesame oil
- 1/4 cup low sodium soy sauce
- 1 tablespoon light brown sugar
- 1/8 teaspoon. ground ginger
- Pinch red pepper flakes
- 2 tablespoon green onions, chopped

Instructions:

1. Chop head of cauliflower into florets and place in food processor. Pulse until it starts to resemble rice; set aside.
2. Heat a large skillet over medium heat and drizzle in sesame oil. Add onion, peas and carrots and sauté until tender.
3. Meanwhile in a small bowl, whisk together soy sauce, brown sugar, ginger and red pepper flakes Set aside.
4. Push the vegetables to one side of the skillet, and tip in beaten eggs and scramble. When eggs are cooked stir it in with the vegetables.
5. Add in the cauliflower "rice" and pour the soy sauce over top. Cook while stirring until cauliflower is soft and tender.
6. Top with green onions, serve and enjoy!

Chickpea Shawarma Stuffed Pita

Cook Time: 35 min
Servings: 2

Ingredients:

- 3 cloves garlic, minced
- 1 tablespoon ground cumin
- 1 tablespoon ground coriander
- 1 teaspoon sea salt
- 1 teaspoon turmeric powder
- 1 teaspoon allspice
- ½ teaspoon ground ginger
- ½ teaspoon ground black pepper
- Pinch of cayenne pepper

- 3 tablespoons olive oil
- 2 cups chickpeas, cooked
- ⅓ cup thinly sliced red onion
- 1/4 cup thinly sliced red pepper
- 2 pita with pockets
- 1/4 cup hummus
- 1 to 2 handfuls chopped lettuce
- Feta, optional
- Parsley, for topping

Instructions:

1. Preheat oven to 400° F. In a medium bowl, combine the garlic with spices (cumin through the cayenne pepper). Drizzle in the olive oil and stir until well a paste forms.
2. Stir in the chickpeas, red onions, and red pepper, use a spatula to coat the chickpeas with the paste. Transfer chickpeas to a roasting pan and cover with aluminum foil. Bake for 30 minutes until chickpeas are roasted and onions are tender.
3. Slice each pita in half and heat the pita until soft. Open the pocket and spread hummus on one side. Stuff with a handful of lettuce and 1/4 of the chickpea mixture. Repeat with remaining pita halves.
4. Serve with extra hummus, parsley, and feta if desired.

Chicken Taco Pizza

Cook Time: 1 hour 25 min
Servings: 3

Ingredients:

1/4 cup canola oil, plus more for brushing
1 packet of taco seasoning
1 pound skinless, boneless chicken breasts
1 16-ounce tube pizza dough
All-purpose flour, for dusting
1 cup shredded mozzarella
1 cup shredded sharp cheddar
1 avocado

Juice of 1 lime
1/2 teaspoon ground cumin
1/2 teaspoon chili powder
1 tablespoon diced red onion
Kosher salt and freshly ground black pepper
1 cup fresh salsa
1/2 cup sour cream
1/4 cup chopped fresh cilantro

Instructions:

1. Make the taco seasoning: Mix all of the ingredients with 1 tablespoon each salt and black pepper in a bowl.
2. Prepare the pizza: Mix 2 tablespoons of the taco seasoning and the canola oil in a shallow bowl. Pound the chicken between 2 pieces of plastic wrap until about 1/4 inch thick. Add the chicken to the bowl and coat with the seasoning. Marinate for at least 30 minutes.
3. Preheat a grill to medium high and grill the chicken until cooked through. Let the chicken cool before cutting into bite-size pieces.
4. Divide the pizza dough into 3 pieces. Roll out each on a floured surface into a small round. Brush dough with canola oil and sprinkle with taco seasoning. Frill until crisp and then remove from the grill.
5. Mix the cheeses in a bowl and then sprinkle on the crusts. Top pizza with the chicken and return the pizzas to the grill. Grill until the cheese has melted.
6. Meanwhile make the salsa. In a bowl, mix the avocado, lime juice, cumin, chili powder, red onion. Season with salt and pepper to taste. Top the pizzas with the avocado mixture, salsa, sour cream and cilantro

Chicken Parmesan

Cook Time: 55 min
Servings: 6

Ingredients

- 1/2 cup unseasoned wholegrain breadcrumbs
- 2 tablespoons grated parmesan cheese
- 1 teaspoon Italian seasoning
- 1/2 teaspoon granulated garlic
- 1/2 teaspoon onion powder
- 1/2 teaspoon salt
- 1/2 teaspoon ground pepper
- 1 tablespoon olive oil
- 2lbs chicken cutlets
- 3/4 cup sauce
- 3/4 cup mozzarella cheese

Instructions

1. Preheat oven to 375 degrees.
2. In a medium bowl mix together the breadcrumbs, parmesan cheese, granulated garlic, onion powder, salt, and pepper.
3. Coat a sheet pan with the olive oil.
4. Dredge each chicken cutlet in the breadcrumb mixture and place on the sheet pan. Discard the rest of the breadcrumb mixture.
5. Bake the chicken for 15 minutes. Turn over and bake for another 15 minutes.
6. Remove the pan from the oven and spread 2 tablespoons of sauce and 2 tablespoons of shredded mozzarella cheese on each chicken cutlet.
7. Place back in the oven and cook for 10 - 15 minutes or until sauce is hot and cheese is melted.
8. Serve hot.

Salmon with Green Peppercorn Sauce

Cook Time: 20 min
Servings: 4

Ingredients:

- 4 salmon filets, skinless and boneless
- 1/4 teaspoon plus a pinch of salt
- 2 teaspoons canola oil
- 1/4 cup lemon juice
- 4 teaspoons unsalted butter, cut into small pieces
- 1 teaspoon green peppercorns in vinegar, rinsed and crushed

Instructions:

1. Sprinkle salmon pieces with 1/4 teaspoon salt. Heat oil in a large nonstick skillet over medium-high heat. Add the salmon and cook until the flesh flakes easily with a fork.
2. Remove the salmon from the skillet and add lemon juice, butter, peppercorns and a pinch of salt. Swirl the skillet so the ingredients are coated with the butter. Cook on medium low heat until the butter turns a light golden brown and fragrant.
3. To serve, top each portion of fish with about two teaspoons of sauce.
4.

Easy Tuna Sliders

Cook Time: 20 min
Servings: 8

Ingredients:

- 35 ounces canned tuna, thoroughly drained
- 1 bunch scallion, thinly sliced
- 1 red bell pepper, diced
- 2 eggs, beaten
- 8 whole wheat hamburger buns
- 1/2 cup mayonnaise
- 2 tablespoons garlic
- 1 tablespoon lemon juice

Instructions:

1. Sautee garlic in pan until brown.
2. Combine garlic, lemon juice and mayonnaise.
3. Combine tuna, scallions, bell pepper and eggs in a bowl.
4. Separate tuna mixture into 8 patties and grill patties until fish is completely cooked.
5. Put a patty on each sandwich with about a tablespoon of the mayonnaise mixture

Sausage and Cauliflower Casserole

Cook Time: 40min
Servings: 4

Ingredients:

- 1 head of cauliflower, cut into florets
- 1 tablespoon extra-virgin olive oil
- 8 ounces Italian sausage, casings removed
- 1 medium yellow onion, diced
- 5 cloves garlic, minced
- 4 sprigs thyme
- 1 can whole peeled tomatoes
- 1/2 cup almond flour
- 2 tablespoon fresh parsley, chopped
- Salt and pepper, to taste

Instructions:

1. Bring a pot of water to boil. Add the cauliflower florets to the pot and boil for 3 minutes. Drain and rinse the florets with cold water. Set aside.
2. Preheat the oven to 350 F. Heat the olive oil in a large skillet over medium-high heat. Add the sausage and cook until sausage turns brown, and then break into small pieces with a wooden spoon.
3. Stir in the onion, garlic, and thyme. Sauté, stirring regularly. Add the tomatoes with juices to the pan and cook for an additional 5 minutes. Season with salt and pepper to taste.
4. Remove the skillet from heat and carefully stir in the cauliflower. Transfer the mixture to a baking dish. Sprinkle the top with almond flour and bake for 20 minutes.
5. At the end, broil and cook until the top is golden brown. Garnish with parsley to serve.

Rainbow Garden Pasta Salad

Cook Time: 40 min
Servings: 4

For the Salad:

- 1 pint cherry tomatoes, halved
- 6 medium carrots, diced (about 1 cup)
- 1 large yellow bell pepper, diced (about 1 cup)
- 4-5 stalks celery, diced 6 medium carrots, diced (about 1 cup)

- ¼ small red onion, diced (about ¼ cup)
- ⅓ cup chopped flat leaf parsley
- 1 pound cooked and cooled elbow pasta, or pasta shape of choice (whole wheat or gluten free)

For the Dressing:

- 1 teaspoon Italian seasoning (or dried oregano)
- ½ teaspoon garlic powder

- 1 teaspoon salt
- ¼ cup red wine vinegar
- ¾ cup extra virgin olive oil

Instructions:

1. In a small bowl, add the Italian seasoning, garlic powder, salt and vinegar. Slowly drizzle in the olive oil and whisk until well combined.
2. In a large bowl, combine the cooked pasta, tomatoes, carrots, bell pepper, celery, red onion, and parsley. Pour over the dressing and gently toss to combine. Let the salad rest for 30 minutes for the flavors to meld before serving.

Pesto Zoodles

Cook Time: 15 min
Servings: 2

Ingredients

- 1 garlic clove, minced
- ⅓ cup raw, unsalted pumpkin seeds
- ¼ cup nutritional yeast
- ½ teaspoon salt
- 2 cups packed mint or basil leaves
- Juice of half a lemon
- ⅔ cup extra virgin olive oil
- 1 teaspoon honey
- 4 zucchinis, spiralized
- 1 pint cherry tomatoes, halved

Instructions:

1. Combine the garlic, seeds, nutritional yeast, salt, lemon juice, basil or mint, and honey in a food processor and pulse until coarsely chopped.
2. Drizzle in the olive oil, processing until smooth. Season with salt and pepper to taste.
3. Toss zoodles with the pesto and let sit for 5 minutes for the zoodles to absorb the sauce and soften a bit. Toss again and serve immediately to avoid the zoodles getting mushy.

Potato and Green Bean Salad

Cook Time: 40 min
Servings: 4

Ingredients

1 ½ pounds small baby potatoes
1 pound green beans, trimmed and cut into 1-inch pieces
1 small shallot, very thinly sliced
1 garlic clove, minced
2 tablespoons honey

1 tablespoon yellow mustard
½ teaspoon salt
¼ cup red wine vinegar
⅓ Cup extra virgin olive oil
¼ cup chopped flat leaf parsley

Instructions

1. Drop the potatoes into a large pot of boiling salted water and cook until they are soft but not falling apart, about 20 minutes. Strain and set aside. Reserve the boiling water from the potatoes to cook the green beans. Boil the beans until just cooked and bright green. Drain and rinse with cold water.

2. Make the dressing by whisking together the garlic, honey, mustard, salt, and red wine vinegar in a small bowl. Drizzle in the olive oil at the end and continue to whisk until incorporated.

3. When the potatoes are cool enough to handle, slice them into bite-sized pieces. Add the sliced potatoes, green beans and shallots to a large bowl. Pour over the dressing and toss to combine. Let the salad sit for at least 10 minutes for the flavors to meld.

4. Sprinkle with parsley just before serving.

Slow Cooker Chicken and Quinoa Stew

Cook Time: 4 hours
Servings: 6

Ingredients

- 1 medium yellow onion, chopped
- 3 garlic cloves, minced or finely grated
- 3 large carrots, chopped
- 1 teaspoon Italian seasoning
- 2 teaspoons salt
- 1 15-oz can tomato sauce
- 1 15-oz can chickpeas, drained and rinsed
- 1 pound boneless, skinless chicken breasts or thighs
- 32 ounces chicken stock
- 2 cups water
- 1 cup fresh or defrosted frozen corn kernels
- 1 medium zucchini, chopped
- ½ cup quinoa, rinsed
- 1/4 cup fresh parsley for serving (optional)

Instructions

1. Add the onion, garlic, carrots, Italian seasoning, salt, tomato sauce, chickpeas, stock, and water to a slow cooker. Stir gently to mix the ingredients. Add the chicken on top of the vegetables.
2. Cover and cook on high for 3.5 hours.
3. Remove the chicken and shred with two forks and set aside. Add the corn, zucchini, and quinoa. Cover and continue to cook on high for an additional 30 minutes, or until the quinoa is cooked.
4. Add in shredded chicken, sprinkle with parsley and serve.

Grilled Portobello Mushroom Burgers

Cook Time: 1 hour 30 min
Servings: 6

Ingredients:

- 6 whole wheat buns, toasted
- 6 large Portobello mushrooms caps of about 5 inches diameter, cleaned
- 2 cloves garlic, minced
- 6 slices red onion
- 6 slices tomatoes
- 3 bib lettuce leaves, halved
- 1/2 cup balsamic vinegar
- 3 tablespoons olive oil
- 1 1/2 tablespoons sugar
- 3/4 cup water
- 1/2 teaspoon cayenne pepper

Instructions:

1. Place the mushrooms in a glass dish with the stem area facing up.
2. Mix together, in a bowl, vinegar, water, sugar, garlic, cayenne pepper and oil. Pour over the mushrooms. Cover and refrigerate for at least an hour. Flip the mushrooms over half way through in the refrigerator.
3. Prepare a charcoal grill or preheat a broiler. Remove the grill rack and spray the rack with cooking spray. Place the rack at least 4 inches away from the heat source.
4. Grill or broil the mushrooms over medium heat. Turn the mushrooms over a couple of times. Grill until the mushrooms are tender. Baste the mushrooms with the remaining marinade.
5. Place a mushroom over each of the buns. Layer tomato and onion slices on top of the mushrooms. Finish with a lettuce leaf and top of the other half of the bun.

Hearty Jambalaya

Cook Time: 6 hours 15 min
Servings: 2

Ingredients:

- 1 can (14 ounce) tomatoes, diced, with its juices
- 1/2 pound fully cooked turkey sausage, cubed
- 1/2 pound chicken breasts, boneless, skinned, cut into 1 inch cubes
- 4 ounce canned tomato sauce
- 1/2 cup onions, diced
- 1/2 a small red bell pepper diced
- 1/2 a small green bell pepper, diced
- 1/2 cup chicken broth
- 1 celery stalk, leaves, chopped
- 1 tablespoon tomato paste
- 1 teaspoon dried oregano
- 1 teaspoon Cajun seasoning
- 1 teaspoon garlic, minced
- 1 bay leaf
- 1/2 pound medium shrimp, cooked
- 1 teaspoon hot sauce
- Hot cooked rice to serve

Instructions:

1. Add all the Ingredients into a pressure cooker except the shrimp and rice. Cover.
2. Set the cooker on low for 6-7 hours or until the chicken is cooked through.
3. Add shrimp. Cover and cook again for 15 minutes. Discard bay leaves.
4. Serve hot over the hot rice.

The Green Pasta

Cook Time: 25 min
Servings: 2

Ingredients:

- 6 ounce uncooked, whole wheat pasta
- 3 cups fresh broccoli florets without stem
- 3 cloves garlic, minced
- 2 tablespoons parmesan or Romano cheese, grated
- 1 tablespoon olive oil, divided
- Salt to taste
- Freshly cracked pepper powder to taste

Instructions:

1. Place a large pot of water to boil. Add 1-teaspoon salt and pasta. When the pasta is almost cooked, add broccoli. Cook until the pasta is al dente. Drain the pasta. Retain about 1 cup of the cooked water.
2. Return the pot back to heat. Add ½ tablespoon oil. When heated, add garlic and sauté until golden.
3. Lower heat and add the drained pasta and broccoli. Mix well. Add the remaining olive oil and cheese. Mix well. Add the retained cooking water, salt and pepper.
4. Heat well and serve hot.

Easy Zucchini Pizza

Cook Time: 15 min
Servings: 1

Ingredients:
- 1 large zucchini, sliced into 1/4 inch thick slices
- Cooking spray
- Pepper to taste
- 1/2 cup pizza sauce
- 1/4 cup part skim mozzarella cheese, shredded

Instructions:
1. Spray the zucchini slices with olive oil on both the sides. Sprinkle salt and pepper.
2. Place the zucchini slices in a preheated broiler at 500 degree F for 2 minutes. Flip sides and broil for another 2 minutes.
3. Remove from the broiler. Spread pizza sauce over each of the slice and sprinkle cheese. Broil for a couple of minutes until the cheese is melted.
4. Serve hot.

Chicken Tikka Masala

Cook Time: 4 hours
Servings: 2

Ingredients:

- ½ of a 15 ounce can crushed tomatoes
- 1 onion, chopped
- 2 cloves garlic
- 1 tablespoon tomato paste
- 1 teaspoon garam masala (Indian spice powder)
- ¾ pound boneless chicken thighs

- 2 tablespoons cilantro, chopped
- ½ tablespoon fresh lemon juice
- ½ cup long grain white rice,
- ½ teaspoon salt
- ¼ teaspoon pepper powder
- ¼ cup low fat cream

Instructions:

1. Add crushed tomatoes, onion, garlic, tomato paste, gram masala, salt and pepper to the slow cooker.
2. Lay chicken thighs on top of the vegetables. Set the slow cooker on Low for 7-8 hours or on High for 3-4 hours.
3. Meanwhile, cook rice according to the instructions on the package. When the chicken done add the cream, stir well.
4. Garnish with cilantro and serve with hot rice.

Zucchini Pad Thai

Cook Time: 30 min
Servings: 2

For the sauce:
- 3/4 tablespoon coconut sugar
- 1 teaspoon Sriracha sauce or to taste
- 2 tablespoons tamarind paste
- 2 teaspoons low sodium tamari
- 1 tablespoon lime juice
- 2 tablespoons low sodium chicken stock

For the noodles:
- 1 large carrots, peeled, trimmed with top and bottom sliced off
- 2 large zucchini, trimmed with top and bottom sliced off

For Pad Thai:
- 1 1/2 cups bean sprouts
- 1 large skinless boneless chicken breast, sliced
- 1 egg, beaten
- 2 teaspoons olive oil, divided
- 1 green onion, thinly sliced
- 2 tablespoons peanuts, finely chopped
- Lime wedges to serve
- Salt to taste
- Pepper powder to taste

Instructions:

1. To make noodles: Make noodles out of the carrot and zucchini by using a spiralizer or a julienne peeler.
2. For pad Thai: Place a nonstick pan over medium heat. Add 1/2-teaspoon oil. When oil is heated, add egg, salt and pepper. Keep stirring so as to scramble it. Remove from the pan when cooked and place it in a bowl.
3. Place a large nonstick pan over medium heat. Add remaining oil. When oil is heated, add chicken breasts, salt and pepper. Cook until the chicken is tender inside and golden brown outside. Place it along with the egg.
4. To make sauce: Add all the Ingredients of the sauce to a bowl and mix well. Place the pan back on heat. Pour the sauce mixture into the pan and cook until it is bubbly.
5. Add zucchini and carrot noodles and cook sauté for a few minutes until it is thoroughly heated and slightly softened. Add chicken, eggs, and sprouts. Mix well and heat thoroughly.
6. Garnish with lemon wedges, green onion and peanuts and serve immediately.

Creamy Lemony Baked Macaroni

Cook Time: 40 min
Servings: 6

Ingredients:

- 1 pound extra-lean ground beef
- 1 large onion, diced
- 14 ounces whole-wheat elbow macaroni, cooked
- 2 jars (15 ounce each) low sodium spaghetti sauce
- 3/4 cup Parmesan cheese

Instructions:

1. Place a large nonstick pan over medium heat. Add onions and sauté for a few minutes until the onions are translucent.
2. Add beef and cook until brown. Add pasta and spaghetti sauce. Mix well and transfer into a greased baking dish.
3. Bake in a preheated oven at 350 F for about 30 minutes.
4. Serve garnished with Parmesan cheese.

Healthy Brown Rice Pilaf

Cook Time: 45 min
Servings: 4

Ingredients:

- 2 1/4 cup brown rice, rinsed, drained
- 4 cups water
- 1 1/2 teaspoon salt
- 1/4 teaspoon saffron threads
- 1/4 teaspoon ground turmeric
- 1 teaspoon orange zest
- 6 tablespoons fresh orange juice
- 3 tablespoons canola oil
- 1/2 cup pistachio nuts, chopped
- 1/2 cup dried apricots, chopped

Instructions:

1. Place a large saucepan over high heat. Add rice, water, 1/2-teaspoon salt, saffron, and turmeric. Cook until the rice is done.
2. Transfer the cooked rice to a large bowl.
3. Mix together orange zest, orange juice, oil and remaining salt. Whisk well. Pour this over the cooked rice. Add nuts and apricots and toss well.
4. Serve immediately.

Soba Noodles with Mushroom

Cook Time: 30 min
Servings: 4

Ingredients:

- 1/4 cup canola oil
- 2 shallots, minced
- 2 carrots, finely chopped
- 4 cloves garlic, minced
- 3 tablespoon fresh ginger, minced
- 17 ½ Ounces white or brown mushrooms, sliced
- 2 cups frozen edamame, thawed
- 3 cups low sodium broth (vegetable or chicken)
- 1/4 cup low sodium soy sauce
- 2 teaspoons lemon zest, grated
- 2 cups spinach, rinsed, chopped
- 1 cup firm tofu, cut into 1/2 inch pieces
- 1/2 teaspoon freshly ground pepper
- 12 1/3 ounces soba noodles

Instructions:

1. Bring a large pot of water to boil. Add the soba noodles. Cook until al dente.
2. Drain. Rinse with cold water. Set aside.
3. Meanwhile place a large nonstick pan or wok over medium heat. Add canola oil.
4. Add shallot, ginger and garlic and sauté for a minute. Add carrot and mushrooms. Stir well. Reduce heat, cover, and cook until the mushrooms are soft.
5. Uncover and increase the heat to medium. Add edamame and sauté until thoroughly heated.
6. Add broth, soy sauce, and lemon zest and bring to a boil. Add spinach. Sauté until spinach wilts. Add tofu, salt, and pepper. Stir and remove from heat. Add the boiled soba noodles and toss well
7. Serve hot in bowls.

Shrimp and Artichoke Angel Hair Pasta

Cook Time: 25 min
Servings: 2

Ingredients:

- 1 tablespoon grape seed oil
- 1 medium onion, diced small
- ½ cup mushrooms, thinly sliced
- 2 garlic cloves, thinly sliced
- ½ cup canned artichokes, quartered
- 2 ½ cups chicken broth
- 6 ounce raw angel hair pasta, broken in half
- ½ cup raw shrimps, peeled, deveined
- ½ teaspoon dried oregano
- A pinch crushed red pepper flakes (optional)
- ½ cup fresh spinach roughly chopped
- Salt to taste
- Pepper to taste

Instructions:

1. Heat oil in a pot over medium heat. When oil is hot, add onions, mushrooms, and garlic. Sauté for a couple of minutes and add artichokes, chicken broth, pasta, shrimps, oregano, red pepper flakes, salt, and pepper.

2. Mix well and bring to a boil. Cover and cook until the pasta is al dente. Add spinach and cook for a couple of minutes until the spinach wilts.

3. Adjust the seasonings if required. Serve hot.

Summer Vegetable Rice

Cook Time: 25 min
Servings: 2

Ingredients:

- 1 tablespoon vegetable oil
- 2 onions chopped
- 2 teaspoons ground ginger
- 1 teaspoon turmeric powder
- 1 teaspoon cumin seeds
- 4 cups mixed vegetables, chopped (vegetables of your choice like cauliflower, carrots, peas, etc.)
- 2 large potatoes, peeled, diced
- 2 cups brown rice, soaked in water for at least an hour
- 1 teaspoon salt
- 5 cups water
- 1 can kidney beans

Instructions:

1. Heat a large skillet over medium heat. Add oil. When oil is hot, add cumin and heat until fragrant. Add onion. Sauté for a couple of minutes. Add ginger and turmeric, sauté for a minute.
2. Add rest of the Ingredients stir and bring to a boil. Lower heat. Cover, and cook until rice is done.
3. Serve hot.

Easy Mushroom Chili

Cook Time: 45 min
Servings: 2

Ingredients:

- 1 tablespoon vegetable oil
- 1/2 cup onions, chopped
- 1/2 tablespoon garlic, minced
- 1 tablespoon chili powder
- 1/2 teaspoon ground cumin
- 3/4 pound white button mushrooms, sliced
- 4 ounce shiitake mushrooms, sliced
- 1/2 a 14 1/2 ounce can stewed tomatoes
- 1/2 a 19 ounce can white kidney beans, rinsed, and drained
- 1/4 cup sliced ripe olives
- 2 tablespoon cheddar cheese, shredded

Instructions:

1. Place a saucepan over medium heat. Add oil. When the oil is heated, add onions and garlic. Sauté until the onions are translucent.
2. Add chili powder and cumin and sauté for a few seconds. Add the mushrooms and sauté for a few minutes until the mushrooms are tender.
3. Add tomatoes, white beans, olives, and about 1/2-cup water. Simmer for about 10 minutes.

Basil Pesto Stuffed Mushrooms

Cook Time: 30 min
Servings: 4

Ingredients:
- 20 cremini mushrooms, washed and stems removed
- 1 1/2 cups panko breadcrumbs
- 1/4 cup melted butter
- 3 tablespoons chopped fresh parsley

For the Filling:
- 2 cups fresh basil leaves
- 1/4 cup fresh Parmesan cheese
- 2 tablespoons pumpkin seeds
- 1 tablespoon olive oil
- 1 tablespoon fresh garlic
- 2 teaspoons lemon juice
- 1/2 teaspoon kosher salt

Instructions:
1. Preheat the oven to 350 F.
2. Line the mushroom caps, rounded side down, onto a baking sheet.
3. In a small bowl, combine the panko, butter and parsley; set aside and prepare the stuffing.
4. Place the basil, cheese, pumpkin seeds, oil, garlic, lemon juice and salt in a food processor. Pulse until the ingredients are evenly mixed, but not pureed. Stuff the mushroom caps with the basil pesto filling.
5. Sprinkle each mushroom with about 1 teaspoon of panko topping. Pat down the topping and bake for 10 to 15 minutes or until golden brown.

Easy Coconut Shrimp

Cook Time: 25 min
Servings: 2

Ingredients:
- 1/4 cup sweetened coconut
- 1/4 cup panko breadcrumbs
- 1/2 teaspoon kosher salt
- 1/2 cup coconut milk
- 12 large shrimp, peeled and deveined

Instructions:
1. Heat the oven to 375 F. Coat a baking sheet lightly with cooking spray.
2. Put the coconut, panko and salt in a food processor and pulse. In a small bowl pour in the coconut milk.
3. Dip each shrimp first into the coconut milk and then into the panko mixture. Place on to the greased baking sheet.
4. Lightly spray the tops of the shrimp with cooking spray. Bake about 10 to 15 minutes until golden brown.

Simple and Delicious Pizza Margherita

Cook Time: 1 hour 25 min
Servings: 2

For the dough:

- 1 teaspoon active dry yeast
- 3/4 cup warm water
- 3/4 cup whole-wheat flour
- 2 tablespoons barley flour
- 2 teaspoons gluten
- 1 tablespoon oats
- 1 tablespoon olive oil

For the Toppings:

- 2 1/2 cups chopped spinach
- 2 1/2 cups sliced tomatoes
- 1/4 cup chopped basil
- 1 tablespoon minced oregano
- 1 tablespoon minced garlic
- 1 teaspoon black pepper
- 2 ounces fresh mozzarella

Instructions:

1. Activate the yeast according the package directions. Combine dry ingredients.
2. Mix oil and yeast mixture and knead for 10-15 minutes for best texture. Put dough in refrigerator to rise for at least 1 hour.
3. Preheat the oven to 450 F.
4. Roll out dough ball on to a floured surface, about 1/4-inch in thickness. Put dough on baking sheet or pizza peel.
5. Top with spinach, tomatoes, basil, oregano, garlic, black pepper and mozzarella.
6. Bake for 10-12 minutes or until the cheese melts and crust is crisp.

Chicken and Spanish Baked Rice

Cook Time: 25 min
Servings: 2

Ingredients:

- 1 cup onions, chopped
- 3/4 cup sweet green peppers
- 2 teaspoons vegetable oil
- 1 cup tomato sauce
- 1 teaspoon parsley, chopped
- 1/4 teaspoon black pepper
- 1-1/2 teaspoon garlic, minced
- 1 cup cheddar cheese
- 5 cups white rice, cooked in unsalted water
- 3-1/4 cup chicken breast, cooked (skin and bone removed), diced

Instructions:

1. In a large skillet sauté onions and green peppers for about 5 minutes on medium heat. Mix tomato sauce and spices. Bring to a boil.
2. Add chicken breast and heat through.
3. Pour sauce over cooked rice. Sprinkle cheese on top and bake in a preheated oven at 350 F for 10-15 minutes, or until the cheese is golden brown and bubbly.

Coconut Quinoa Curry

Cook Time: 3 hours 15 min
Servings: 2

Ingredients:

- 1 medium sweet potato, peeled + chopped (about 3 cups)
- 2 cups of fresh green beans (cut into ½ inch pieces)
- 1 medium size carrot (cut into small bit size pieces)
- ½ white onion, diced (about 1 cup)
- 1 (15 oz.) can organic chickpeas, drained and rinsed
- 1 (28 oz.) can diced tomatoes
- 2 (14.5 oz.) cans coconut milk (either full fat or lite)
- ¼ cup quinoa
- 2 garlic cloves, minced (about 1 tablespoon)
- 1 tablespoon freshly grated ginger
- 1 tablespoon freshly grated turmeric (or 1 teaspoon ground)
- 2 teaspoon tamari sauce
- ½ - 1 teaspoon chili flakes
- 1 - 1½ cups water

Instructions:

1. Pour 1 cup of water into a slow cooker. Put all ingredients to the slow cooker.
2. Stir to incorporate everything fully.
3. Turn slow cooker to high and cook for 3 - 4 hours until sweet potato cooks through and the curry has thickened.
4. Serve as a vegetarian soup or over rice

Simple and Delicious Shepherd's Pie

Cook Time: 45 min
Servings: 4

Ingredients:

- 2 large baking potatoes, peeled and diced
- 1/2 cup low-fat milk
- 1 pound lean ground beef
- 1 medium onion, chopped
- 1 clove garlic, minced
- 2 tablespoons flour
- 4 cups frozen mixed vegetables
- 3/4 cup reduced sodium beef broth
- 1/2 cup shredded cheddar cheese
- Ground pepper to taste

Instructions:

1. Put diced potatoes in saucepan and add enough water to cover. Bring to a boil.
2. Turn down the heat and simmer the potatoes, covered, until soft (about 15 minutes). Drain potatoes and mash. Mix in milk, and set mixture aside.
3. Preheat oven to 375 degrees.
4. In a large skillet brown meat, onion, and garlic. Stir in flour, and cook for 1 minute, stirring constantly. Pour in broth. Cook until thick and bubbly, stirring occasionally.
5. Spoon the mixture into an 8 inch square baking dish. Spread the mashed potatoes over vegetable/meat mixture. Sprinkle cheese on top.
6. Bake 25 minutes, until hot and bubbly.

Pumpkin Lasagna

Cook Time: 40 min
Servings: 4

Ingredients:

- 2 tablespoons olive oil
- 2 onions, chopped
- 2 pounds Swiss chard, tough stems removed, leaves washed well and chopped
- 2 1/4 teaspoons salt
- 1 teaspoon fresh-ground black pepper
- 1 teaspoon dried sage
- 1/2 teaspoon grated nutmeg
- 3 cups canned pumpkin puree (one 28-ounce can)
- 1 1/2 cups heavy cream
- 1 1/2 cups grated Parmesan
- 1/2 cup milk
- 9 no-boil lasagna noodles (about 6 ounces)
- 1 tablespoon butter

Instructions:

1. In a skillet, heat the oil and then add the onions. Sauté until translucent and fragrant. Increase the heat and then sauté the chard with, salt, 1 pepper, sage, and nutmeg. Cook, while stirring, until the chard has wilted and the skillet is has no liquid remaining.
2. Preheat the oven to 400 F. In a medium bowl, combine the pumpkin, cream, Parmesan, and the remaining seasonings.
3. Pour the cream mixture into a baking dish. Top with a third of the noodles, and then spread half the pumpkin puree over the noodles. Layer half the Swiss chard on top and repeat this combination until all ingredients are done, reserve 1 cup of pumpkin puree and 3/4 cup of cream. Spread this mixture over the top of the pasta.
4. Sprinkle with Parmesan. Cover the baking dish with aluminum foil and bake for 20 minutes.
5. Uncover and bake until golden, about 15 minutes more.

Chicken Salad with Creaming Tarragon Dressing

Cook Time: 20 min
Servings: 4

Ingredients:

- 15 ounces canned white beans
- 1/3 cup White Balsamic Vinegar
- 1 tablespoon extra-virgin olive oil
- 2 garlic clove
- 2 tablespoon tarragon, fresh, divided
- 6 cups Salad Mix

- 1/2 medium red onion, thinly sliced
- 1 1/3 cups Chicken Breast, Cooked, chopped
- 12 Grapes (Red or Green), thinly sliced
- 1 cup English Cucumber, thinly sliced
- 3 tablespoon pine nuts
- 3/4 teaspoon ground black pepper

Instructions:

1. Add 1/2 cup of the beans, the vinegar, oil, garlic, and 1 tablespoon. Of the tarragon to a blender. Cover and puree.
2. Arrange greens on a large platter. Top with remaining beans, onion, chicken, grapes, cucumber, nuts, pepper, and remaining 1 tablespoon tarragon.
3. Serve the dressing on the side.

Spinach-Stuffed Turkey Burger Patties

Cook Time: 30 min
Serves: 4

Ingredients:

- 12 oz. Ground Turkey 93% Lean
- 3 cups Fresh Baby Spinach
- 1/3 cup Old Fashioned Rolled Oats
- 1 garlic clove, minced
- 1 egg(s), beaten
- 2 tsp 100% Lemon Juice
- 3/4 tsp ground black pepper
- 1/2 tsp sea salt
- 1 pinch Nutmeg (Ground)

Instructions:

1. In a medium bowl, combine all of the ingredients.
2. Spray a large nonstick skillet with cooking spray and place over medium heat. Form mixture into 4 (5-inch wide) patties and cook in the skillet until well done and browned, about 7 to 8 minutes per side.

Summer Squash Rice

Cook Time: 30 min
Servings: 5

Ingredients:

- 2 tablespoons olive oil
- 1 small onion, finely chopped (about 1 1/4 cups)
- 1 red bell pepper, cut into 1/2-inch cubes
- 1 medium yellow zucchini or crookneck squash, cut into 1/2-inch cubes
- 1 medium green zucchini, cut into 1/2-inch cubes
- 1 1/2 cups long-grain white rice (about 10 ounces)
- 3 cups low-salt chicken broth
- 3 tablespoons roasted salted shelled pumpkin seeds
- 3 tablespoons finely chopped Italian parsley

Instructions:

1. Heat oil in large saucepan over medium-high heat.
2. Add onion and cook until soft, stirring frequently. Add bell pepper, yellow zucchini, and green zucchini; sauté until vegetables begin to soften, Add rice; sauté for about 1 minute, stirring constantly. Sprinkle with salt and pepper.
3. Add broth and increase heat to high, bring to boil. When boiling, reduce heat to low, cover, and cook until rice is tender, 18 to 20 minutes.
4. Season to taste with salt and pepper. Turn off heat and stir in pumpkin seeds and parsley.

Zucchini Lasagna

Cook Time: 45 min
Servings: 6

Ingredients:

- 1 tablespoon olive oil
- 2 large zucchinis, sliced about 1/4-inch thick
- 4 large tomatoes, sliced about 1/4-inch thick
- 2 medium onions, sliced very thin
- 1 sprig fresh basil, 6-8 leaves, chopped
- 8 ounces shredded mozzarella
- Ground black pepper

Instructions:

1. Grease a medium casserole dish with olive oil. Cover the bottom of the dish with sliced zucchini. Then, spread a layer of tomatoes and a layer of onions.
2. Top with half of the sliced basil and season with ground pepper. Sprinkle a layer of about half the shredded cheese.
3. Keep layering the vegetables and the cheese until none is left.
4. Bake in an oven preheated to 400 F for about 30 minutes. Let cool for 5 minutes before serving

Spicy Baked Spinach and Cod

Cook Time: 2 min
Servings: 2

Ingredients:

- Cooking oil spray
- 1 pound cod (or other fish) fillet
- 1 tablespoon olive oil
- 1 teaspoon spicy seasoning mix

Instructions:

1. Preheat oven to 350 degrees. Spray a casserole dish with cooking spray.
2. Wash the fish and pat dry. Place the fish into the casserole dish and sprinkle with oil and seasoning mix.
3. Bake uncovered for 15 minutes or until fish flakes with fork.
4. Cut the fishes into 4 pieces. Serve with rice.

Black Bean Salad Stuffed Sweet Potato

Cook Time: 30 min
Servings: 2

Ingredients:

- Vegetable oil
- 2 large sweet potatoes, pricked
- 1 teaspoon salt
- 1/2 teaspoon freshly ground black pepper
- 1/4 cup fresh lime juice, plus wedges for garnish
- 1 tablespoon balsamic vinegar
- 1 tablespoon finely chopped garlic

- 1 can (15 ounces) black beans, rinsed and drained
- 1 cup halved cherry tomatoes
- 1/2 cup thinly sliced orange or red bell pepper
- 1/2 cup thinly sliced scallions
- 1/3 cup chopped fresh mint
- 4 cups baby arugula

Instructions:

1. Rub the sweet potatoes with oil and season with salt and pepper; bake in an oven preheated to 375 F. Bake until tender, 15-25 minutes; let cool.
2. In a bowl, whisk juice, vinegar, garlic. Season with salt and pepper. Add beans, tomatoes, bell pepper, scallions and mint; toss.
3. To serve, slice a sweet potato in half, length wise and lightly mash the insides. Fill the sweet potato with the bean salad. Top with arugula, and garnish with lime wedges.

Meal Prep Dessert Recipes

Mango Tapioca Rice Pudding

Cook Time: 50 min
Servings: 2

Ingredients:

- 1 1/2 cup low fat milk
- 1/2 cup rice
- 1/4 cup tapioca
- 2 tablespoons coconut sugar
- 1/2 teaspoon vanilla extract
- 5 -6 drops almond extract
- A large pinch of cinnamon
- 1 mango, cubed
- 2 tablespoons almonds, toasted, chopped

Instructions:

1. Place a heavy saucepan over medium heat. Add milk, tapioca and rice. Bring to a boil.
2. Lower heat and simmer until the rice is cooked.
3. Remove from heat. Add sugar, vanilla extract, and cinnamon. Stir in mangoes.
4. Serve either warm or cold sprinkled with almonds and more mango cubes on top. Keep in an airtight container in the refrigerator for up to 3 days.

Apple Pudding Cake

Cook Time: 4 hours
Servings: 4

Ingredients:

- 4 cups apple, cored, finely chopped (do not peel)
- 4 cups coconut sugar
- 4 cups flour
- 4 eggs
- 2 cups vegetable oil
- 2 cups walnuts, chopped
- 2 teaspoons baking soda
- 1 teaspoon nutmeg, grated

Instructions:

1. Mix together in a bowl, flour, nutmeg, and baking soda. Add sugar, oil, eggs and vanilla to a large bowl and beat well. Add the dry ingredient mixture and mix well. Add apples and fold.
2. Grease the inside of the slow cooker. Pour the batter into the cooker.
3. Slip a toothpick between the lid and the slow cooker to create a gap for excess steam. Do not open lid until cooking time is done.
4. Set the cooker on High for 3 1/2 to 4 hours. Slice when warm or cold and serve with a sweet sauce of your choice (optional).

Holiday Pumpkin Pie

Cook Time: 1 hour
Servings: 6

Ingredients:

- 2 cups ginger snaps, ground
- 32 ounces canned pumpkin
- 1 cup egg whites
- 1 cup coconut sugar
- 4 teaspoons pumpkin pie spice blend
- 2 cans (12 ounce each) evaporated skim milk

Instructions:

1. Grease an ovenproof pie pan with cooking spray. Place the ground cookies in the pan. Spread well and press lightly.
2. In a large bowl, mix together the rest of the Ingredients. Pour over the cookies.
3. Bake in a preheated oven at 350 degree F for about 40-45 minutes.
4. Cool and refrigerate for up to 4 days. Slice into wedges and serve.

Pear Caramel Pudding

Cook Time: 1 hour 15 min
Servings: 4

Ingredients:

- 1 cup all-purpose flour
- 1/3 cup granulated sugar
- 1 tablespoon flaxseed meal
- 1 teaspoon baking powder
- A pinch salt
- ½ teaspoon cinnamon powder
- ½ cup fat free milk
- 2 tablespoons canola oil
- ¼ cup dried pears, snipped
- ½ cup water
- ½ cup pear nectar
- 6 tablespoons brown sugar
- 1 tablespoon butter
- Fat free vanilla yogurt (optional)
- Cooking spray

Instructions:

1. In a bowl mix together flour, granulated sugar, flaxseed meal, and baking powder, cinnamon, and salt. Add milk and oil. Mix well. Add the dried pears.
2. Spray the inside of the slow cooker with cooking spray. Pour the batter into the cooker.
3. Meanwhile mix together water, pear nectar, brown sugar, and butter in a saucepan. Heat it and bring to a boil. Boil for 2 minutes.
4. Pour this sugar solution over the batter in the cooker. Cover. Set the cooker on low for 3 1/2 hours.
5. When done, switch off the cooker. Uncover and let it remain in the cooker for about 45 minutes.
6. Divide into bowls. Serve topped with yogurt.

After Dinner Chocolate Pudding

Cook Time: 30 min
Servings: 2

Ingredients:

- 6 tablespoons cornstarch
- 4 tablespoons cocoa powder
- 4 tablespoons coconut sugar or to taste
- 1/8 teaspoon salt
- 4 cups nonfat milk
- 2/3 cup chocolate chips
- 1 teaspoon vanilla

Instructions:

1. In a large saucepan, whisk together milk, cornstarch, cocoa, sugar, and salt.
2. Place the saucepan over medium heat. Stir constantly until the mixture thickens.
3. Remove from heat and add chocolate chips and vanilla. Mix well until the chocolate chips are dissolved.
4. Pour into individual serving bowls. Cover with cling film. Keep aside to cool. Refrigerate until use.

Sunday Chocolate Banana Cake

Cook Time: 40 min
Servings: 4

Ingredients:

- 2 cups all-purpose flour
- 1/2 cup Splenda Brown Sugar Blend
- 1/4 cup unsweetened cocoa powder
- 1/2 teaspoon baking soda
- 1 large ripe banana, mashed (1/2 cup)
- 3/4 cup soy milk
- 1/4 cup canola oil
- 1 large egg
- 1 egg white
- 1 tablespoon lemon juice
- 1 teaspoon vanilla extract
- 1/2 cup semisweet dark chocolate chips

Instructions:

1. Preheat oven to 350 F. Spray the bottom of an 11 x 7 inch brownie pan with nonstick spray.
2. In a large bowl combine together flour, brown sugar blend, cocoa, and baking soda.
3. Whisk together the bananas, soy milk, oil, egg, egg white, lemon juice, and vanilla in another bowl.
4. Make a hole in the middle of the flour mixture. Pour soy milk mixture and chocolate chips into the hole.
5. Stir the ingredients together with a wooden spoon, until combined. Tip the batter into the pan.
6. Bake about 25 minutes until the center of the cake springs back when pressed lightly with fingertips.

Summer Fresh Fruit Kebabs

Cook Time: 15 min
Servings: 2

Ingredients:

- 6 ounces low-fat, sugar-free lemon yogurt
- 1 teaspoon fresh lime juice
- 1 teaspoon lime zest
- 4 pineapple chunks (about 1/2 inch each)
- 4 strawberries
- 1 kiwi, peeled and quartered
- 1/2 banana, cut into 4 1/2-inch chunks
- 4 red grapes
- 4 wooden skewers

Instructions:

1. Whisk the yogurt, lime juice and lime zest in a small bowl.
2. Cover and chill in the refrigerator until needed.
3. Thread the one of each fruit onto a skewer. Repeat until all the fruit has been skewered.
4. Serve with the lemon lime dip.

Baked Brie Envelopes

Cook Time: 25 min
Servings: 4

Ingredients:

- 1/2 cup fresh or frozen cranberries
- 1/2 medium orange, quartered
- 2 tablespoons sugar
- 1 cinnamon stick
- 1 sheet puff pastry dough, cut into 12 1/4-ounce squares
- 6 ounces Brie cheese, cut into 1/2-ounce cubes
- 2 tablespoons water
- 1 egg white

Instructions:

1. Preheat oven to 425 F. Coat a small sauce pan with cooking spray and heat on medium-high heat
2. In the pan add the oranges, cranberries, sugar and cinnamon stick, and cook for about 10 minutes. Stir constantly until cranberries are soft and the mixture starts to thicken. Remove from heat and let it cool. Remove orange quarters and the cinnamon stick.
3. Roll out each square of puff pastry. Onto each puff pastry square, place 1 teaspoon of cooled cranberry mixture and one cube of cheese.
4. Combine the water and egg white in a small bowl. Dab a small amount of the egg mixture onto the edges of the puff pastry.
5. Fold one corner of the pastry at a time around the cheese and cranberry mixture, like an envelope.
6. Baste the top of the pastry with the egg mixture. Place the envelopes on a baking sheet and bake for 10 to 12 minutes or until golden brown.

Almond and Sour Cherry Chocolate Bark

Cook Time: 1 hour (for chocolate to set)
Servings: 24

Ingredients:

- 3/4 cup almonds, toasted and unsalted
- 12 ounces dark chocolate (60 percent to 70 percent cocoa)
- 1/2 teaspoon pure vanilla extract
- 1/3 cup dried tart cherries, roughly chopped

Instructions:

1. Fill a medium saucepan with 2 inches of water; bring to a simmer over medium-low heat. Place a slightly larger heatproof bowl on top of the saucepan, making sure water doesn't touch bottom of bowl.
2. Place 10 ounces dark chocolate (60 percent to 70 percent cocoa) in bowl and stir, until smooth. Remove bowl from saucepan; add another 2 ounces dark chocolate and stir until smooth.
3. Stir in 1/2 teaspoon pure vanilla extract, toasted almonds and 1/3 cup dried tart cherries. Pour onto baking sheet and spread into an even layer about 1/4 inch thick.
4. Refrigerate until firm, 1 hour. Break into 24 pieces.

Chocolate-Mint "Nice Cream"

Servings: 1

Ingredients:

- 1 banana, frozen
- 1 tbsp. Unsweetened Cocoa Powder
- 1/2 tsp peppermint extract

Instructions:

1. Portion ingredients into sandwich bags.

2. When ready to use, place all ingredients into a high-powered blender and blend until smooth and creamy. Serve immediately.

Mango and Macadamia

Servings: 1

Ingredients:

1 frozen medium banana
1/2 cup frozen mango pieces
1 tablespoon maple syrup

5-6 macadamias, chopped
1/2 cup coconut milk

Instructions:

1. Portion ingredients into sandwich bags.

2. When ready to use, place all ingredients into a high-powered blender and blend until smooth and creamy. Serve immediately.

Low Fat Brownies

Cook Time: 30 min
Servings: 16

Ingredients:

- 6 ounces semisweet chocolate
- 1/2 cup hot water
- 4 egg whites
- 1 teaspoon vanilla extract

- 2/3 cup granulated sugar
- 1 1/2 cups all-purpose flour
- 1 teaspoon baking powder
- 1/2 cup chopped walnuts (optional)

Instructions:

1. Melt chocolate in a large heatproof bowl set over simmering water; stir until smooth. Remove from heat and let cool slightly. Whisk in egg whites and followed by the vanilla.
2. In a separate bowl, mix together the sugar, flour, and baking powder; stir into chocolate batter until just combined. Fold in walnuts.
3. Spray an 8-inch cake pan with cooking spray. Pour batter into cake pan and bake in an oven preheated to 350 F for 20-25 minutes, or until edges pull away from pan.
4. Let the brownies cool slightly on a cooling rack, then slice and serve.

Decadent Oatmeal and Banana Cookies

Cook Time: 25 min
Servings: 18

Ingredients:

- 4 ripe bananas
- 1/4 cup Palm sugar (coconut sugar)
- 1 1/2 cups old fashioned oats
- 1/2 cup dried cherries
- 1/2 cup dark chocolate chips
- Pinch of ground nutmeg
- 1/2 tsp cinnamon

Instructions:

1. Preheat oven to 350 F and line a cookie sheet with parchment paper.
2. In medium bowl mash bananas. Add the rest of the ingredients and mix well.
3. Drop batter onto the prepared cookie sheet and bake for about 10 minutes, or until the bottoms of the cookie are golden brown.

Three Layer Chia Pudding Parfait

Cook Time: 30 min
Servings: 2

For the Chia Layer:
- 1/2 cup chia seeds
- 1 1/2 cups coconut milk

For the Green Layer:
- 2 frozen bananas
- 1 kiwi
- 4-inch piece of cucumber
- Handful of baby spinach
- 1/2 cup coconut milk

For the Berry Layer:
- 2-3 tablespoon oats
- Frozen blueberries
- Fresh strawberries
- 2 frozen bananas
- 1/2 cup coconut milk

Instructions:

1. Make chia pudding layer by combining chia seeds with coconut milk. Stir well and let sit covered for at least 20 minutes in fridge or overnight.
2. Make green layer by blending the bananas, kiwi, cucumber, spinach and coconut milk. Freeze until ready to use.
3. Make the pink layer. Add oats, blueberries, strawberries and bananas to a blender and blend until smooth. Divide the mixture into two jars.
4. When ready to serve, add chia pudding on top of the berry layer and spoon the green layer on top. If green layer has frozen overnight, blend for a few seconds on high in a blender.
5. Garnish with blackberries, or other fruit, before serving.

Gooey Matcha Lava Cakes

Cook Time: 20 min
Servings: 2

Ingredients:

- 4 ounces white chocolate
- 1/2 cup unsalted butter
- 1 cup confectioner's sugar
- 2 whole eggs
- 2 egg yolks
- 6 tablespoon all-purpose flour
- 1 tablespoon matcha green tea powder

Instructions:

1. Melt the butter and white chocolate in a microwave safe bowl in 30-second intervals until smooth. Make sure to stir in between each interval. Add the confectioner's sugar and stir to until well combined.
2. Whisk in the eggs and egg yolks until smooth.
3. In a separate bowl, combine the flour and matcha green tea powder. Stir. Whisk the dry ingredients into the wet ingredients until there are no lumps.
4. Grease two ramekins and place on top of a baking sheet for easy clean up. Portion the mixture evenly between the ramekins and bake in a preheated oven at 425F for 13-15 minutes, or just until the edges are firm and the center jiggles slightly when shaken.
5. If serving immediately, let cool for 2 minutes before using a knife to separate the cake edges from the ramekins, and then turn out onto a dish. Cakes can be frozen for up to a couple days and then reheated in an oven.

Meal Prep Snack Recipes

Chocolate Matcha Energy Balls

Cook Time: 10 min
Servings: 10

Ingredients:

- 1/2 cup soft pitted dates* (make sure they are sticky)
- 1/2 cup raw almonds
- 1/4 cup unsweetened cocoa powder
- 1 tablespoon matcha green tea powder + more for dusting
- 1 tablespoon unsweetened almond milk

Instructions:

1. Add dates and almonds to a food processor and process until they comes together. Add in cocoa powder, matcha powder, and almond milk to loosen up the mixture. Mixture should have a thick ganache consistency.
2. Portion mixture to form 10 servings and roll into balls with the palm of your hands. If mixture is too sticky, chill in the refrigerator for a while. Dust the balls with more matcha powder.
3. Store in refrigerator for up to 2 weeks or longer in freezer.

Lemon and Vanilla Energy Balls

Cook Time: 10 min
Serves: 20

Ingredients

- 1 cup raw almonds
- 1 cup pitted dates
- 1/2 cup vanilla protein powder
- 2 teaspoon maca powder
- 1/2 teaspoon sea salt
- Zest, 1 lemon
- Juice, 1/2 lemon

Instructions

1. Add almonds to a food processor and process until it reaches a crumbly consistency.
2. Add in dates, protein powder and maca powder and process until combined.
3. Add in sea salt, lemon zest and juice and continue processing until mixture comes together into a thick, sticky, ball.
4. Portion into 20 pieces and roll pieces into balls.
5. Store in refrigerator for several weeks or longer in freezer.

Peanut Butter Cup Energy Bites

Cook Time: 10 min
Serving: 14

Ingredients

- 3/4 cup raw almonds
- 1 teaspoon raw cocoa powder
- 12 pitted dates
- 2 tablespoon peanut butter

Instructions

1. Place almonds in a small food processor and pulse until your almonds are finely chopped but not powdery. Set aside.
2. Process the pitted dates until they become like a paste. Then, add the rest of the ingredients, including the chopped almonds. Process for an additional minute.
3. Portion mixture into bite-sized pieces and roll into balls with the palm of your hands. Store in the refrigerator for a couple weeks or longer in the freezer.

Apple Pie Energy Balls

Cook Time: 10 min
Servings: 15

Ingredients

- 1 cup pitted dates
- 1 cup unsweetened dried apple rings, chopped
- 1/2 cup rolled oats, gluten-free if necessary
- 1 cup cashews
- 1 teaspoon cinnamon
- 1/4 teaspoon nutmeg
- 1/4 teaspoon sea salt

Instructions

1. In a food processor, add the cashews, dates, and apple rings until it comes together to form a sticky ball.
2. Add in the oats, spices, salt, and pulse until well combined and mixture is sticky.
3. Portion mixture and roll into balls with the palm of your hands.
4. Store for up to a couple weeks in the refrigerator or longer in the freezer.

Crunchy Maple Chai Roasted Chickpeas

Cook Time: 50 min
Servings: 6

Ingredients:

- 2 cups chickpeas, drained, rinsed, dried
- 1 tablespoon olive oil
- 1 tablespoon. pure maple syrup
- 1/2 teaspoon. ground ginger
- 1/2 teaspoon. ground cinnamon
- 1/4 teaspoon. ground cardamom
- 1/4 teaspoon. ground cloves
- 1/4 teaspoon. sea salt (or Himalayan salt)
- 1/4 teaspoon. ground black pepper

Instructions:

1. Preheat oven to 400 F.
2. In a large bowl, gently toss the chickpeas with oil, maple syrup, ginger, cinnamon, cardamom, cloves, salt, and pepper.
3. Spread chickpeas on large baking sheet in a single layer and bake for 35 to 38 minutes. Make sure the shake the baking sheet every 10 minutes, to ensure even cooking.

Homemade Energy Bars

Cook Time: 10 min
Servings: 12

Ingredients:

- 1 cup whole pitted dates
- 1 cup dried fruit (such as apricots, blueberries, cranberries etc.)
- 1 cup chopped nuts or seeds (such as almonds, cashews, sunflower seeds, etc.)
- 2 scoops protein powder, any flavor

Instructions:

1. Place dates, fruit, and nuts in a food processor. Pulse for 1 to 2 minutes, scraping down the sides of the bowl every so often.
2. Add in your protein powder and continue to process for 2 to 3 minutes, or until mixture becomes sticky and crumbly.
3. Line a shallow pan with plastic wrap. Press mixture into pan until flat. Cover tightly and refrigerate for 1 hour. Cut into 12 bars.
4. Store in refrigerator for up to one week.

Turkey Snack Roll-Ups

Prep Time: 5 min
Servings: 1

Ingredients

- 1 slice uncured organic deli ham (or use any ham you wish)
- 1 tablespoon hummus
- 1/2 slice Swiss cheese
- 4-5 baby spinach leaves

Instructions

1. Spread hummus onto the slice of ham. Top with Swiss cheese and spinach leaves.

2. Roll up and enjoy.

Easy Everyday Hummus

Cook Time: 10 min
Servings: 4

Ingredients:

- 2 cans (16 ounces each) reduced-sodium garbanzos, rinsed and drained except for 1/4 cup liquid
- 1 tablespoon extra-virgin olive oil
- 1/4 cup lemon juice
- 2 garlic cloves, minced
- 1/4 teaspoon cracked black pepper
- 1/4 teaspoon paprika
- 3 tablespoons tahini (sesame paste)
- 2 tablespoons chopped Italian flat-leaf parsley

Instructions:

1. Add the garbanzo beans in a blender or food processor and puree until smooth.
2. Mix the olive oil, lemon juice, garlic, pepper, paprika, tahini and parsley and blend well.
3. Pour the reserved liquid into the mixture, 1 tablespoon at a time until the mixture has the consistency of a thick spread.
4. Serve instantly or cover and chill it in refrigerator until ready to serve.

Roasted Red Pepper Hummus

Cook Time: 5 min
Servings: 4

Ingredients:

- 2 cups chickpeas
- 1 cup roasted red bell pepper, slices, seeded
- 2 tablespoons white sesame seeds
- 1 tablespoon lemon juice
- 1 tablespoon olive oil

- 1 1/4 teaspoons cumin
- 1 teaspoon onion powder
- 1 teaspoon garlic powder
- 1 teaspoon kosher salt
- 1/4 teaspoon cayenne pepper

Instructions:

1. Put together all the ingredients in a food processor.

2. Process until smooth.

Meal Prep Smoothie and Juice Recipes

Berry Lemon Smoothie

Ingredients:

- 1 cup blueberries, chopped
- 1 cup strawberries, chopped
- 1 cup blackberries, chopped
- 1 cup lemon juice
- 1/2 cups plain yogurt
- ½ teaspoon salt
- 2 tablespoons sugar
- Mint leaves
- Ice cubes

Instructions:

1. Portion all ingredients except the yogurt and lemon juice into sandwich bags and freeze.
2. When ready to use, pour the sandwich bag contents into a blender with the yogurt and lemon juice. Loosen smoothie with water or nut milk if too thick.

Berry and Oatmeal Milkshake

Ingredients:

- 1 cup regular oatmeal
- 1 cup strawberries, chopped
- 1 cup blueberries chopped
- 1 cup full cream milk
- 1 large banana, chopped
- 2 tablespoons sugar
- Mint leaves
- Ice cubes

Instructions:

1. Portion all ingredients except the milk into sandwich bags and freeze.

2. When ready to use, pour the sandwich bag contents into a blender with the milk. Loosen smoothie with water nut milk if too thick.

Raspberry Pineapple Mint Juice

Ingredients:

- 1 cup pineapple, chopped
- 1 cup raspberries, chopped
- 1 cup lemon juice
- ½ teaspoon salt

- 1 tablespoon honey
- 1 cup mint leaves
- Ice cubes

Instructions:

1. Add the pineapple to the juicer and extract the juice.
2. Add the raspberries to the juicer and extract the juice.
3. Add the two to a pitcher and mix until well combined.
4. Add in the lemon juice and mix well.
5. Add in salt and honey and mix until well combined.
6. Add in the mint leaves and use a muddler to crush it gently.
7. Add the ice cubes and mix.
8. Serve cold.

Raspberry Grape Juice

Ingredients:

- 1 cup grapes, chopped
- 1 cup raspberries, chopped
- 1 cup lemon juice
- ½ teaspoon salt
- 1 tablespoon honey
- Mint leaves
- Ice cubes

Instructions:

1. Add the grapes to the juicer and extract the juice.
2. Add the raspberries to the juice and extract the juice.
3. Combine the two in a pitcher and mix.
4. Add in the lemon juice and mix until well combined.
5. Toss in the salt and stir.
6. Add in the honey and mix until well combined.
7. Add in chopped mint leaves and ice cubes and mix.
8. Serve cold.

Raspberry Lychee Mint Juice

Ingredients:

- 1 cup lychees, chopped
- 1 cup raspberries, chopped
- 1 cup orange juice
- ½ teaspoon salt
- 1 tablespoon honey
- 1 cup mint leaves
- Ice cubes

Instructions:

1. Add the lychees to the juicer and extract the juice.
2. Add the raspberries to the juicer and extract the juice.
3. Add the two to the pitcher and mix until well combined.
4. Add in the orange juice and mix well.
5. Add the salt, and honey and mix until well combined.
6. Add the mint leaves and use a muddler to extract the flavor.
7. Add in ice cubes and mix well.
8. Serve cold.

Blackberry and Orange Juice

Ingredients:

- 1 cup blackberries, chopped
- 1 cup oranges, chopped
- 1 cup lemon juice
- ½ teaspoon salt
- 1 tablespoon honey
- Mint leaves
- Ice cubes

Instructions:

1. Add the blackberries to a juicer and extract the juice.
2. Add the oranges to a juicer and extract the juice.
3. Add the two to a pitcher and add in the lemon juice.
4. Mix and toss in the salt.
5. Add in the honey and mint leaves and use a muddler to crush the mint leaves.
6. Add in the ice cubes and stir.
7. Serve cold.

Blueberry Smoothie

Ingredients:

- 2 cups blueberries, chopped
- 1 cup banana, chopped
- 2 cups plain yogurt
- ½ teaspoon salt
- 2 tablespoons honey
- Mint leaves
- Ice cubes

Instructions:

1. Add the blueberries to a blender along with the banana and yogurt and whizz until smooth.
2. Add in the salt and honey and whizz further.
3. Add in the ice cubes and whizz further.
4. Serve with a sprinkling of mint leaves.

Blueberries and Orange

Ingredients:

- 1 cup oranges, chopped
- 1 cup blueberries, chopped
- 1 cup orange juice
- ½ teaspoon salt
- 1 tablespoon honey
- Mint leaves
- Ice cubes

Instructions:

1. Add the oranges to a juicer and extract the juice.
2. Add the blueberries to the juicer and extract the juice.
3. Combine the two in a pitcher and well combine.
4. Add in the orange juice and mix until well combined.
5. Add the salt, honey and chopped mint leaves and use a muddler to crush the mint.
6. Add in ice cubes and stir.
7. Serve cold.

Apple Berry Juice

Ingredients:

- 1 cup frozen mixed berries
- 1 cup apples, chopped
- 1 cup pears, chopped
- ½ teaspoon salt

- 1 tablespoon honey
- Mint leaves
- Ice cubes

Instructions:

1. Add the apples to a juicer and extract the juice.
2. Add the fresh apple juice to a blender along with frozen berries and chopped pears, blend until mixed.

3. Pour into a pitcher stir in the salt and honey and mint leaves. Add in ice cubes and mix well. Serve cold or keep refrigerated.

Apple Sparkling Grape Juice

Ingredients:

- 1 cup apples, chopped
- 3 cups green grapes
- 1 cup orange juice
- 1 cup sparkling water
- 1 lemon, juiced
- Mint leaves
- Ice cubes

Instructions:

1. Add the apples to the juicer and extract the juice.
2. Add the grapes to the juicer and extract the juice.
3. Add them to a pitcher along with the orange juice and sparkling water. Mix until well combined.
4. Squeeze in the lemon juice and mix.
5. Chop the mint leaves and add to the pitcher.
6. Add in the ice cubes and mix until well combined

Melon and Pear Smoothie

Ingredients:

- 1 cup pear, chopped
- 1 cup watermelon, chopped
- 1 cup musk melon, chopped
- 1 large banana, chopped
- 2 cups plain yogurt
- ½ teaspoon salt
- 2 tablespoons sugar
- Mint leaves
- Ice cubes

Instructions:

1. Add the pear, watermelon, muskmelon, banana and yogurt to a blender and whizz until well combined.
2. Add in the salt and sugar and whizz further.
3. Add the ice cubes and blend.
4. Serve cold with a sprinkling of mint leaves.

Melon and Coconut Water

Ingredients:

- 1 cup musk melon, chopped
- 1 cup coconut water
- 1 cup oranges, chopped
- ½ teaspoon salt
- 1 tablespoon honey
- Mint leaves
- Ice cubes

Instructions:

1. Add the muskmelon to a juicer and extract the juice.
2. Add the oranges to a juicer and extract the juice.
3. Combine the two in a pitcher and mix until well combined.
4. Add in the salt and honey and mix well.
5. Add the mint leaves and use a muddler to crush it.
6. Add in ice cubes and mix well.
7. Serve cold.

Melon and Carrot Juice

Ingredients:

- 1 cup carrots, chopped
- 1 cup melon, chopped
- 1 cup coconut water
- ½ teaspoon ginger, chopped

- ½ teaspoon salt
- 1 tablespoon honey
- 1 cup mint leaves
- Ice cubes

Instructions:

1. Add the carrots to a blender and extract the juice.
2. Add the melon to a juicer and extract the juice.
3. Add both to a pitcher and mix until well combined.
4. Add in the ginger and mint leaves and crush to release flavor.
5. Add the salt and honey and mix until well combined.
6. Add in the ice cubes and stir.
7. Serve cold.

Spicy Melon Juice

Ingredients:

- 1 cup watermelon chopped
- 1 cup pineapple, chopped
- 1 cup lemon juice
- 1 green chili, deseeded
- ½ teaspoon salt
- 1 tablespoon honey
- Mint leaves
- Ice cubes

Instructions:

1. Add the melon to a blender and whizz.
2. Add the pineapple to a juicer and extract the juice.
3. Add both to a pitcher and mix.
4. Toss in the lemon juice, chili, salt, honey and mix until well combined.
5. Add in the mint leaves and use a muddler to crush and release flavor.
6. Mix in the ice cubes.
7. Serve cold.

Watermelon and Coconut Water Juice

Ingredients:

- 1 cup watermelon, chopped
- 1 cup orange juice
- 1 cup coconut water
- ½ teaspoon salt
- Mint leaves
- Ice cubes

Instructions:

Add the watermelon to the juicer and juice.

Add in the orange juice and blend until well combined.

Add to a pitcher along with the coconut water and stir until well combined.

Add in the salt and mix.

Add the chopped mint leaves and combine.

Toss in the ice cubes and mix well.

Serve cold.

Aloe Very and Coconut Juice

Ingredients:

- 1 cup aloe vera, chopped
- 1 cup coconut water
- 1 cup lemon juice
- ½ teaspoon ginger, chopped
- ½ teaspoon salt
- 1 tablespoon honey
- 1 cup mint leaves
- Ice cubes

Instructions:

Use a sharp knife to cut open an aloe vera leaf and remove the transparent sap from in between.

Add to a blender along with the coconut water and well combine.

Add to a pitcher along with the lemon juice, salt and honey and mix well.

Add in the ginger and use a muddler to crush and release flavor.

Add in the mint leaves and ice cubes and well combine.

Serve cold.

Mango Green Tea Milkshake

Ingredients:

- 1 cup mangoes, chopped
- 1 cup warm water, chopped
- 1 green tea bag
- 1 cup full cream milk
- 1 large banana, chopped
- 2 tablespoons sugar
- Mint leaves
- Ice cubes

Instructions:

1. Add the warm water to a cup and place the green tea bag in it.
2. Allow it to steep for some time.
3. Meanwhile, add the mango, banana to a blender along with the cream and sugar and whizz until smooth.
4. Add in the tea and whizz further.
5. Add in the ice cubes and blend.
6. Serve cold with mint leaves on top.

Mango Milkshake

Ingredients:

- 2 cups mango, chopped
- 2 cups full cream milk
- ½ teaspoon salt
- 2 tablespoons honey
- Mint leaves
- Ice cubes

Instructions:

1. Add the mangos to a blender along with the milk and whizz until well combined.
2. Add to a pitcher along with the salt and honey and mix until well combined.
3. Add in the ice cubes and mix.
4. You can also add in crushed ice.
5. Serve cold with a sprinkling of mint leaves on top.

Mango Peach Smoothie

Ingredients:

- 1 cup frozen mangoes
- 1 cup peaches, chopped
- 1 large banana, chopped
- 2 cups plain yogurt
- ½ teaspoon salt
- 2 tablespoons honey
- Mint leaves
- Ice cubes

Instructions:

1. Add the peach and mangoes to a blender along with the banana and yogurt and whizz until smooth.
2. Add in the salt and honey and blend until well combined.
3. Toss in the ice cubes and blend.
4. Serve cold with a sprinkling of mint leaves on top.

Mango and Chili Juice

Ingredients:

- 1 cup mangoes, chopped
- 2 red chilies, deseeded
- 1 cup lemon juice
- ½ teaspoon salt

- 1 tablespoon honey
- Mint leaves
- Ice cubes

Instructions:

1. Add the mango to a blender and blend until well combined.
2. Add to a pitcher along with the lemon juice and mix until well combined.
3. Add in the chilies and use a muddler to crush.
4. Toss in the salt and honey and combine.
5. Add the mint leaves and mix well.
6. Add ice cubes and stir.
7. Serve cold.

Tamarind and Tomato Juice

Ingredients:

- 2 tablespoons tamarind pulp
- 1 cup tomatoes, chopped
- ½ teaspoon ginger, chopped
- ½ teaspoon salt
- 1 tablespoon sugar
- 1 cup mint leaves
- Ice cubes

Instructions:

1. Add the tamarind pulp and tomato to a blender and mix until well combined.
2. Add in the ginger, salt, sugar and whizz until smooth.
3. Add to a glass along with the mint and crush.
4. Add ice cubes and serve cold.

Beetroot Pomegranate Juice

Ingredients:

- 1 cup beetroot, chopped
- 1 cup coconut water
- 1 cup pomegranate, deseeded
- ½ teaspoon salt
- 1 tablespoon honey
- 1 cup mint leaves
- Ice cubes

Instructions:

1. Add the beetroot to a juicer and extract the juice.
2. Add the pomegranate and extract the juice.
3. Combine both in a pitcher.
4. Add in the salt, honey and mix until well combined.
5. Add the ice cubes and mint and use a muddler to crush the leaves.
6. Serve cold.

Sweet Potato and Celery Juice

Ingredients:

- 1 cup sweet potato, chopped
- 1 cup celery, chopped
- 1 cup lemon juice
- ½ teaspoon ginger, chopped
- ½ teaspoon salt
- 1 tablespoon honey
- 1 cup mint leaves
- Ice cubes

Instructions:

1. Add the sweet potato to a juicer and extract the juice.
2. Add the celery, lemon juice, ginger, salt and honey to a blender and whizz.
3. Add both to a glass along with the potato juice and mix.
4. Add in the ice and serve with a sprinkling of mint leaves on top.

Juice for Healthy Skin

Ingredients:

- 1 cup carrots, chopped
- 2 cups spinach leaves, chopped
- 1 cup apples, chopped
- 1 cucumber, chopped

- 1 teaspoon ginger, chopped
- ½ cup lemon juice
- Mint leaves
- Ice cubes

Instructions:

1. Add the carrots to a juicer and extract the juice.
2. Add the spinach, apples, ginger and lemon juice to a blender and whizz.
3. Combine both in a glass along with the ice and mix.
4. Serve cold with a sprinkle of mint leaves.

Cabbage and Mint Juices

Ingredients:

- 1 cup cabbage leaves, chopped
- 1 cup mint leaves, chopped
- 1 cup lemon juice
- ½ teaspoon ginger, chopped

- ½ teaspoon salt
- 1 tablespoon honey
- 1 cup mint leaves
- Ice cubes

Instructions:

1. Add the cabbage to a juicer and extract the juice.
2. Add in the lemon and mint to a blender and whizz until smooth.
3. Add both to a pitcher and combine.
4. Add in the ginger and mint leaves and crush.
5. Add honey and ice cubes and mix.
6. Serve cold.

Cucumber and Broccoli Juice

Ingredients:

- 1 cup broccoli, chopped
- 1 cup cucumber, chopped
- 1 cup lemon juice
- ½ teaspoon ginger, chopped
- ½ teaspoon salt
- 1 tablespoon honey
- 1 cup mint leaves
- Ice cubes

Instructions:

1. Add the broccoli to a juicer and extract the juice.
2. Add the cucumber to a juicer and extract the juice.
3. Add both to a pitcher along with the lemon juice and mix until well combined.
4. Add in the ginger, and mint leaves and crush to release flavor.
5. Add in the salt and ice cubes and mix well.
6. Serve cold.

Rose Petal and Melon Tea

Ingredients:

- 1 cup rose petals
- 1 cup melon, chopped
- 1 teaspoon ginger
- 1 teaspoon black pepper
- 1 cup of water
- 1 tablespoon honey

Instructions:

1. Add one-cup water to a saucepan and toss in the rose petals.
2. Allow it to boil and release flavor.
3. Meanwhile, add the melon, ginger, pepper and honey to a blender and blend until smooth.
4. Add to a glass and mix in the strained rose water.
5. Serve hot.

Hibiscus and Rose Tea

Ingredients:

- ½ cup hibiscus flowers, chopped
- ½ cup rose petals, chopped
- 1 teaspoon black pepper
- 2 cups of water
- 1 tablespoon honey

Instructions:

1. Add 1-cup water to a saucepan and bring to a boil.
2. Add in the hibiscus and rose petals and allow it to boil.
3. Meanwhile, add the pepper, water and honey to a blender and blend until well combined.
4. Add to a cup along with the strained tea and mix until well combined.
5. Serve hot.

Meal Prep Weekly Meal Plan

Meal Planning is critical to being a successful meal prepper. If you can't plan ahead of what you want to make for the following weeks, then it'll be difficult to organize ingredients, containers, and any prep work. It takes about 5-10 minutes, one day of the week to pick out what meals you have in mind. Here is a simple schedule I've provided for you that'll help you with scheduling your meal prep days. I have also handpicked specific recipes that mixes things up so you and your family won't be bored of similar food types week after week.

I'm making a few assumptions here with this schedule. For example, that you work five days and have 2 days off. I hope that this schedule will at least assist you in having a better idea of how meal prepping works on a daily basis.

My Recommendations:

Week 1:

>Lunch: <u>Creamy Lemony Baked Macaroni</u>
>
>Dinner: <u>Chicken Fajita Bowls</u>
>
>Snack: <u>Berry Lemon Smoothie</u>

Week 2:

>Lunch: <u>Sausage and Cauliflower Casserole</u>
>
>Dinner: <u>Soba Noodles with Mushroom</u>
>
>Snack: <u>Homemade Energy Bars</u>

Week 3:

>Lunch: <u>Simple and Delicious Pizza Margherita</u>
>
>Dinner: <u>Grilled Portobello Mushroom Burgers</u>
>
>Snack: <u>Low Fat Brownies</u>

Week 4:

Lunch: Rainbow Garden Pasta Salad

Dinner: Buddha Bowls

Snack: Berry and Oatmeal Milkshake

Work Day #4

- Write down what meals you want to make on your days off
  - Have ingredients listed out
  - Be aware of what ingredients you have at home

Work Day #5

- Go grocery shopping to get all the ingredients you don't have
- Plan ahead. If you can get things for next week's meal prep, do it
- Stick to your list!
- Get home and organize your food so it is ready for preparation the next day
  - Marinate your meats
  - Defrost you freezer foods
- Prep your ingredients if you have time

Day Off #1

- Prep your ingredients
  - Cut, slice, dice and chop all the ingredients you need
- Start cooking!
  - While cooking, organize your containers and have them ready to receive your portions.
  - Prep sauces and dressings at this stage
- Once cooking is complete, portion size your foods and store the containers away in fridge or freezer

Day Off #2

- Enjoy your day off! Your meal preps are done already.

Work Day #1

- Start eating your meal preps
    - Heat them up appropriately and enjoy the fruits of your labor.
    - Notice what recipes work for you and what doesn't. Adjust for new ingredients or try a whole new recipe.

Work Day #2

- Start brainstorming what to make for next week.
- After two meals, you'll know how your cooking is.
    - If cooking is not your thing, try salads or soups.
    - Get some feedback from the people you cook for and see what they like to eat.

Work Day #3

- Relax! You don't need to think of meal prep every day.
- Repeat this cycle starting tomorrow, Work Day #4

Conclusion

Meal Prep can be made into part of your everyday life. It takes a little bit of commitment and motivation, but once you have the habit down, it means healthy, simple, and on the go meals for you and your family. Hopefully in my book, I have provided you with enough resources so that you can start meal prepping for success! I find that when I meal prep, it becomes a family event. All the members of my family want to know what's for lunch or dinner next week. They also have a lot of opinion on what they want mom to make for them. I love involving them and having them help me prep or cook. It's a great sense of accomplishment for everyone when the last box of meal prep is put away.

I think that it is of utmost importance that I put the right types of fuel in my body and my family's body. Food is life. I want you to live happy and enjoy what you eat!

Happy Meal Prepping!

Made in the USA
Lexington, KY
22 October 2018